CONTENTS

INTRODUCTION

Imagine there's no Heaven. Imagine there's no Hell. Imagine there's no divine revelation or holy commandments. Imagine there's no God, and no religion too. What would this mean? What are the implications of living in a world without supernatural purpose?

It would mean that this life is the only life we have, and that we must make the most of it. It would mean that our understanding and morality are purely human and natural. It would mean that we are responsible for creating our own meaning and value in life. It would therefore mean that we must use human understanding and compassion to make the best of life, for ourselves and for each other. Imagine such a world. . . .

This is the outlook known as "secular humanism." Secular humanists see no convincing evidence for a god or supernatural powers. They believe that we must use human reason and experience to develop moral values that bring out the best in people, so that all people can have the best in life. Secular humanism emphasizes rational and scientific inquiry, individual freedom and responsibility, and tolerance and cooperation.

Many of history's greatest thinkers, artists, scientists and social reformers have been humanists. These freethinkers challenged tradition and went beyond conventional beliefs to expand human understanding and improve society. They imagined a better world, and worked to make their vision a reality.

Great humanists and freethinkers of the past include philosophers from Socrates and Epicurus to Bertrand Russell and Albert Camus, writers and poets such as Percy Bysshe Shelley and Marian Evans ("George Eliot"), scientists such as Charles Darwin and Albert Einstein, social activists such as Elizabeth Cady Stanton and Andrei Sakharov, and political leaders such as

Thomas Jefferson and Pandit Jawaharlal Nehru.

Since its creation in 1980, *Free Inquiry* magazine has been the leading voice of secular humanism. In the pages of *Free Inquiry* you can encounter today's great humanist thinkers as they investigate new areas of human understanding, tackle social and ethical dilemmas, and explore the challenges of living without religion.

Imagine There's No Heaven: Voices of Secular Humanism introduces you to some of these thinkers, with eleven articles and interviews from recent issues of *Free Inquiry*. I hope that these pieces give you an enjoyable and thought-provoking introduction to the breadth and depth of secular humanist thought.

I also hope that *Imagine There's No Heaven* inspires you to support the Council for Secular Humanism—publisher of *Free Inquiry*—in its important work. By becoming an Associate Member of the Council for Secular Humanism you will be joining a community of people who find meaning and value in life without looking to a god. But more than that, you will be able to work with the Council in translating secular humanist ideals into practical actions. (See page 103 for details on becoming an Associate Member of the Council for Secular Humanism.)

In the meantime, good reading!

> Matt Cherry
> Executive Director, Council for Secular Humanism

1

THE NIGHT I SAW THE LIGHT

Gina Allen was the author of several books and articles for adults and juve-niles, including the best-seller Intimacy, *which she coauthored with Clement Martin.*

I first saw the light one night when I was sixteen years old. It was initially a very small light—the beam from the flashlight that enabled me to read under the bedcovers when I was supposed to be sleeping. That night I was reading a Little Blue Book that had been given to me by my boyfriend. It was Percy Bysshe Shelley's *The Necessity of Atheism.*

I usually say that until the moment I opened the book I was a very religious young woman, but I suppose I had actually been outgrowing my religion for a while. For one thing, my boyfriend, a freethinker, had been giving me books like this and had been making me defend my religious beliefs—which I had difficulty doing to his satisfaction, and my own.

So I was prepared for Shelley and his atheism even though I didn't know it. And, as I read, the light got brighter and brighter. Not from the flashlight I was reading with but from my mind absorbing what I read. Shelley's logic shattered, in one memorable night, all the Sunday school lessons, Bible studies, and sermons I had been exposed to for years.

My first reaction was fury, a fury so strong that I risked confronting my father the next morning at breakfast. "You can't possibly believe all that god stuff! Do you?" I demanded. "You're an intelligent, educated man. God is as much a hoax as Santa Claus and not nearly as much fun. And only kids be-lieve in Santa."

His response made me even angrier. This pillar of the religious commu-nity, this trustee of the local Presbyterian church, this man who supported the church financially and attended services every Sunday told me calmly that no, he didn't believe what the church taught. But he did believe that without the church there would be no morality in the world. Children learned right and wrong in the church, and adults lived righteous lives because they believed in God and heaven and hell.

I have since learned that this attitude is not unusual among many who appear to be religious. They are less concerned with their own spirituality than with the conduct of others. They see themselves as superior, able to understand their religion as mythology and still conduct their lives morally. But they don't think the ordinary person can do that, so they count on religion to keep the masses under control. Indeed, throughout history such "superior" men have used religion to regulate their slaves and subjugate women.

In my first heady release from religion I too thought it was the only thing that had kept me "good." My life would change: I could sin. As a teenager, for me the three great sins were smoking, drinking, and premarital sex.

I told my boyfriend that I had seen the light. He was glad. He said he thought I was too intelligent to stay caught up in religion forever. Then I told him that we could sin together. We could drink, and smoke, and have sex. He looked at me as if I were crazy. I could do those things if I wished, he said, but he was in training. As captain of the high-school football team, a star basketball player, and a Golden Gloves boxer, he was always in training.

He wasn't "good" because he believed in a god but because he wanted to be an athlete. Slowly it dawned on me that I hadn't been "good" because I believed in a god but because I loved my family and friends, enjoyed my studies and my music, and wanted to prepare myself for all life's possibilities.

I have never, ever regretted the night I saw the light. I shall be ever grateful to the young athlete who gave me that Little Blue Book (and to the publishers of Little Blue Books). I have stopped being personally furious with the Christian religion that duped me as a child, but I continue to be alarmed at religion when it hurts people, stunts their growth, and practices sexism and racism.

When I visit my family I go to church with them. I cringe through the Apostles' Creed. How narrow and restrictive it is! I cringe through the hymns, too. I'm a pacifist, so "Onward Christian Soldiers" is repugnant. And "Amazing Grace"—which asks God "to save a wretch like me"—shows how destructive religion can be of self-esteem. It spreads guilt instead of joy. It denies nature and closes minds to scientific knowledge.

So except for an annual journey back to my roots in family and the Presbyterian church, I have not returned to religion, nor have I missed it. My associates since the night I saw the light have been people with whom I share common interests and goals, people trying to make this world better, not hoping for heaven. Like Abou Ben Adhem, in Leigh Hunt's wise poem, they are moral because they love this earth and those with whom they share it. I trust they can say the same about me.

2

LOVE OF LIFE: AN INTERVIEW WITH E. O. WILSON

Prolific author and lecturer Edward O. Wilson, now retired, was professor of entomology at the Museum of Comparative Zoology at Harvard University. He is known as the father of sociobiology. The following interview was conducted by FREE INQUIRY *editor Timothy J. Madigan.*

FREE INQUIRY: In your book, *The Diversity of Life,* you state that environmental problems are innately ethical. Could you explain what you mean by this?

EDWARD O. WILSON: Environmental problems are essentially ethical because the solutions we attempt depend on our self-perception as a species, and on the future we envision for ourselves and our descendants. And from these considerations flow our prescription of what is good for humanity and for the environment.

FI: There are some critics of humanism who would say that in fact humanists are only interested in what is good for humanity, and that therefore we look at environmental issues with a sort of crude utilitarianism. In other words, if certain species are not beneficial for human beings then they are expendable. How would you respond to the claim that humanists are only concerned with the environment in regard to how it affects human beings?

WILSON: Humanism can embrace both anthropocentrism, which holds that the fate of the Earth should be determined with reference to what is good for humanity, and biocentrism, which holds, first, that humanity is part of the larger living world and, second, other species have rights which, if not equal to human beings, are still worthy of consideration. I view humanism as probably providing the ultimately soundest basis for an environmental ethics directed to the long-term security of both the world environment and biodiversity within it. The reason is that, having originated by evolution as a species within the living world, we are forever intimately a part of it. It follows that

11

we need to save much of it in a natural state in order to provide ourselves an environment that is physically and psychologically secure.

FI: In the last chapter of *The Diversity of Life* you actually call for a new ethics and speak of the importance of a new approach based upon a naturalistic humanism. What do you mean by this call for a new ethics?

WILSON: I've been attempting to develop the notion of a naturalistic ethics directed to the environment since the publication of *Sociobiology* in 1975. I attempted to test and strengthen the argument in *On Human Nature* in 1978, *Biophilia* in 1984, and now in *The Diversity of Life.* The argument goes essentially as follows: we can understand human nature best and in greatest detail by viewing ourselves as evolutionary products in which the mind, although undeniably unique in the history of evolution, nevertheless has biological roots that can only be understood by references to the deep genetic history of humanity and of our pre-human ancestors. The relationships that we develop toward each other are based on that long history of genetic socialization, and our ethics has arisen from that deep history as well. Therefore, a sound ethics has to take into account our biology and our genetic history, both of which are far more complex and difficult to understand than hitherto appreciated within the traditional venues of moral reasoning. Once deep history has been penetrated and better understood, it should allow a much more objective evaluation of moral codes. This naturalistic approach, which is certainly not new to me but goes back to evolutionary biologists of the nineteenth century, has special applicability in our approach to the environment. It inclines us to recognize that humanity evolved in close association with other life-forms and has an innate tendency to affiliate with them, by the multifarious aesthetic pleasure they provide and the environments— places to live and search—we innately regard as optimal. This affiliation I've called "biophilia," and it is now developing into a serious area of science and scholarship. In the fall of 1993 a book will appear called *The Biophilia Hypothesis,* edited by Stephen Kellert of Yale University and myself, in which authors of different disciplines examine the idea that there is indeed an innate relationship between human beings and the natural environment. If this approach is strengthened by further empirical examination, as I expect it to be, then the naturalistic basis of an environmental ethics should prove to be the soundest one in the long run.

FI: What does "biophilia" literally mean?

WILSON: It means "love of life," and I chose the word to embrace phenomena that might be more appropriately called "biophobia." For example the demonstrated genetically based aversion to snakes has led to the near-universal employment of serpents in metaphor and religious symbolism as objects of power, dread, magic, and veneration. Another example of biophilia that has been studied in some depth includes the ideal environment. There is now a substantial amount of evidence to suggest that human beings respond strongly to certain rather narrowly defined natural environments. Physiological stress as mediated by the autonomic nervous system is reduced most rapidly by the viewing of certain habitats and not others. And the preferred place of residence across many if not most cultures whenever choice can be made—is an African-like savanna, atop a high promontory overlooking water. This may seem farfetched, yet it is borne out by a number of psychological tests and by the evidences of the choice of the rich and powerful around the world, from Park Avenue penthouses to the sites of temples and parliaments in other countries. Consider, if you will, the landscape design and vistas of the most important official buildings and monuments in Washington, D.C.

FI: You stress the connection between ethics and aesthetics, an appreciation of beauty. Does this tie in to your call for a new ethics, that to protect the environment is not simply a matter of cost-benefit analysis, i.e., let's save these particular plants because we might get some medical benefit from them, but also a sense that they are naturally beautiful?

WILSON: I feel that an entire tier of arguments is now sufficiently developed to promote the saving of natural ecosystems, and in virtually every domain that one can think of with reference to long-term planning. They are basically three in number: utilitarian, as a source of food, pharmaceuticals, and other products; ecosystems services, creating and maintaining soil, water, and the very air we breathe; and aesthetic, or in a new sense, spiritual.

FI: You talk about the importance of understanding "biodiversity." Can you explain what you mean by that term?

WILSON: Biodiversity is the sum total of diversity at every level of organization, from the variety of genes within single species, to species (that are the pivotal unit of taxonomic classification), and thence on upward to larger and larger assemblages, to whole ecosystems.

FI: In regard to preserving biodiversity, you make a distinction between a cost-benefit analysis and a safe minimum standard approach to conservation. What is that distinction?

WILSON: One of the fundamental points of disagreement within the domain of environmental ethics is the distinction between the two. Cost-benefit analysis would put a measurable value on these two criteria. Those who attempt it are willing to concede that species mostly have great value, such that the cost of saving them will be outweighed in most instances by the value that we can assign to their preservation. At first, this seems to make sense,

13

because we do operate in a cost-benefit world and it is eminently anthropocentric to think in those terms. But there is a major flaw to the argument, namely that no one has ever been able to fully assess the value of even one species, and the more that species are known as individuals, the more valuable they become from the point of view of their ultimate practical, scientific, and aesthetic potential. When all these things are put together and some attempt is made to imagine how future generations will value them, then the entire exercise becomes futile. And that is the main reason for turning to what is called a "safe minimum standard," which is essentially to do what ever it takes to save every species as a living biological entity, to keep it, preserve it, to allow future generations with greater knowledge (and, we hope, wisdom) to enjoy it and make full use of its enormous potential.

FI: You were calling for the preservation of rain forests long before it became an issue in the popular consciousness. One of the issues that you have been talking about is to locate what you call the world's "hot spots" and protect them.

WILSON: The hot spot concept is very important. Conservationists and biologists recognize that it no longer suffices to identify species here and there that are endangered and to set out to save them. In that respect, the Endangered Species Act of the United States, which has been one of the most enlightened and successful of all pieces of environmental legislation in history, falls short. So many species can still slip through the net it provides, species that are simply not yet recognized as existing, much less being in danger. Furthermore, if we work species by species, the cost of expanding such programs to include all endangered species will become enormous, and we simply don't have time to do it that way in any case. By far, the better procedure is to identify those ecosystems in the world that have the largest number of endangered, endemic species—that is, species found in the particular ecosystems under assault. Then, attempt to save these hot spots. In short, give highest priority to the ecosystems that do contain the largest number of endangered species. We now know that many of the world's hot spots are located in rain forests, and especially the last patches of nearly destroyed rain forests. Rain forests are thought to contain more than half of the species of plants and animals on Earth, even though they only cover about 7 percent of the land's surface, and are disappearing at the rate of about 1.8 percent of their cover each year.

FI: That leads to the topic of human population growth, and the danger it presents to biodiversity. You say in your book that "humanity is ecologically abnormal" in regard to its population growth.

WILSON: No other animal species five kilograms or larger with partly carnivorous habitats has ever come remotely close to present-day humanity in sheer biomass (dry weight of protoplasm). The effects of this profligacy on the environment are staggering. We are co-opting somewhere between 20 percent and 40 percent of the sun's energy fixed by photosynthesis, which means that humans are taking over the area where plants are grown, replacing vegetation with human structures and wasteland. So, we've already greatly diminished the capacity of natural ecosystems to sustain us, and along with this, we are extinguishing the diversity of the world at an accelerating rate. At the present time, I estimate that extinction in the rain forests due to reduction in habitat alone (never mind the components of loss due to the introduction of exotic organisms and partial disturbance of the forests) is in the range of about .5 percent of species annually. Furthermore, the human species has become a geophysical force, as most people are now aware. We are not only reducing the remainder of life in bulk and variety rapidly, we are also altering the very composition of the atmosphere in ways that destroy the protective ozone layer and very probably is warming the Earth's climate with potentially catastrophic effects.

FI: This leads to a problem that you mention in the book. You call it "the awful symmetry," namely that the richest nations preside over some of the smallest biotas, whereas the poorest nations are considered to be the stewards of some of the largest. What sort of challenges does this present?

WILSON: The nations with the greatest biological treasures are the ones least interested in and least able to care for them. This was a major concern at the Rio Conference in June 1992: how to develop a biodiversity treaty that fosters cooperation between north and south. The principles were well spelled out, and, to my relief, biodiversity at long last moved onto the center stage in discussions of the world environment. The Biodiversity Treaty, signed by almost all the nations, agreed to bring some of the wealth, foreign aid, and investment capital from the north into the south for the preservation and use of biodiversity. But I have to admit that practical results have been very meager so far.

FI: In fact, another point you raise is that every nation has an economic and a foreign policy, but the time has come to speak of a population policy.

WILSON: It is astonishing to me that the very idea of population policy still seems to be something of a taboo. Nothing can be more crucial to the future of nations than a population policy, by which I mean a democratic consensus of optimum numbers and geographical distribution. The optimum will depend on the image each country has of itself. Does it wish to be primarily industrial and draw on resources from other countries and depend upon highly efficient trade policies? Would it like to remain primarily agrarian, with large expanses of natural ecosystems? The best population level and with it the ideal geographic distribution will certainly depend in the eyes of its citizenry and the rest of the world on what kind of resources each nation in turn has, what past history has been, its geographic location, and the kind of cooperative arrangements it can can work out with other parts of the world. Countries such as many of those in the Third World with vast resources in biodiversity and year-round growing seasons should seriously consider receding to and maintaining small populations and large expanses of natural areas, both for the health of their people and the economic advantage.

FI: How do you think that the masses of people can be convinced about this? What sort of ways can we really try to change people's views on this topic?

WILSON: By education, of course. And I'm optimistic on those grounds. Realize that we are about to go through a terrible bottleneck in which world population will stabilize or at least slow substantially at somewhere between 10 and 15 billion people, or more than twice the number we have today. Note, too, that energy demands of the developing countries are going to increase enormously. In other words a much greater load is going to be put on the planet's resources and biological diversity than exists today. It's a grim picture. But at the same time there is evidence around the world awakening environmental awareness. The Rio Conference is one example. Here is another: recently, 1,500 of the leading scientists around the world, including a majority of the living Nobelists, issued a warning to the world on these most pressing issues of population and environment. There is a growing perception of the intimate connection between conservation of resources, including biodiversity and economic development, as opposed to the old zero-sum view of conservation versus jobs. And there has been a veritable mushrooming of Green movements around the world in the form of political movements, of new conservation organizations, and cooperative arrangements between business ventures and environmentalist initiatives. So eventually, I believe sooner than later, there will be a sufficient awareness of what the major environmental problems are and what we must do to moderate population growth to save at least a part of the biodiversity and to avoid a great deal of human suffering than would otherwise occur. One of the most encouraging signs that I have seen is the one reported by Robert McNamara in his United Nations address in 1991, namely the estimation that if all of the women in the world, and especially in the developing countries, who wished to have knowledge of and access to birth control but do not yet have it, were in fact given it, the world population would probably stabilize at more than 2 billion less than hitherto projected.

16

FI: Following along that line, are you also optimistic about the influence of a naturalistically based ethics upon existing supernatural belief systems? I'm thinking for example about the Catholic church, which is opposed to promoting knowledge of birth control for very metaphysical reasons.

WILSON: One of the reasons for my optimism is in fact the greening of religion. A great many religious leaders have expressed an interest in incorporating moral reasoning about the environment into their teachings. Last year there was an important meeting held in the United States Senate under the auspices of several key environmentalist senators, including now Vice President Al Gore, in which religious leaders and scientists discussed these problems and the possibility of finding a common moral ground. That included leaders of Judaism, many Protestant denominations, and the Roman Catholic church. This has been something I and other scientists at Harvard have continued to discuss this year with members of the School of Divinity in an ongoing symposium on religion and the environment: that the environment is the one area on the near side of metaphysics (that is, an area in which we can temporarily put aside metaphysics) in which both religious thinkers and humanists can come to an agreement. It should be possible to find common, pragmatic courses of action that have a strong moral underpinning without agreeing on all the metaphysical precepts. I believe also that the leading natalist religions will gradually evolve away from their current position when they see more and more clearly its terrible consequences. Someone once said very wisely that the great problems of history are never solved, they are merely forgotten.

FI: Getting back to what you said earlier in regards to humanists, since they by and large have no problem with accepting the theory of evolution and don't find anything distasteful or upsetting about seeing humans as fully part of a natural setting, what do you think that humanists specifically can do to help in this issue of protecting biodiversity?

WILSON: I think that humanists are exceptionally well qualified to argue a moral basis for saving the environment, for the reasons that I just gave. To summarize, the evolutionary view of human origins connects us far more intimately and solidly with the natural environment than does any other philosophical view of human existence.

FI: I was moved by your statement in *The Diversity of Life* that "every species makes its own farewell to the human partners that have served it so ill." How has the destruction of biodiversity affected you personally?

WILSON: The more I've learned about habitat destruction and species extinction from other scientists, and from my own observations, the greater the sense of urgency and anxiety I've felt. We simply can't wait any longer to do whatever we can to contribute to knowledge and education about the situation. Also, I feel that though they are discouragingly small in number, the humanists in this country nevertheless include a lot of people with convictions about the human responsibility to the biosphere, and they are a potent group.

FI: While we are small in number, we're disproportionate in our influence, and what you talk about in your book are the very sorts of issues we should be getting much more involved with.

WILSON: I agree with you, and I meant what I said earlier, that this is an area where people who are religious and humanists actually can meet. And you may eventually find a partial conversion of theologians and religious leaders due if nothing else to the urgency of the problem. As long as the walls aren't crumbling down around them, they can remain as strictly metaphysical as they want and produce fiats about human reproductive behavior forever, but when things start falling apart and they recognize, as any sane person must, the connection between population expansion, energy use, and potentially catastrophic environmental trends, then they have to adjust. That's the way philosophy and religion have evolved through history.

FI: I suppose we have to hope that they all get revelations from their various gods to tell them to change their metaphysics.

WILSON: Don't be surprised if that happens!

3

THE GODLESS HERO OF AFRICA
AN INTERVIEW WITH TAI SOLARIN

The late Tai Solarin was one of Nigeria's leading educators and social critics. He was the chairman of the People's Bank of Nigeria and a writer for such leading Nigerian newspapers as The Guardian. *He spent much of his life as a human rights activist, and was held in high esteem by many. He was affectionately known as "Uncle Tai" by large numbers of his admirers.*

When I visited Tai's Mayflower School a couple of years ago, I was immediately impressed by the seriousness and dedication of the students. Secular messages stressing the importance of education and self-reliance were posted all over the walls of the school. Everyone seemed inquisitive and eager to learn.

Following is an interview with Dr. Tai Solarin in which he discusses humanism and education in Nigeria.

—Norm Allen, Director
African Americans for Humanism

FREE INQUIRY: What is the Mayflower School, and how did you come up with that name?

TAI SOLARIN: I returned from the United Kingdom in 1952 with bachelors' degrees in history and geography. It was easy for me to be hired as the headmaster of a community school run by local people. But as all schools were run the same way, I was soon queried as to why I was not starting the school day with hymn singing and prayers, and why I was not marching the students—all boys—to the nearby church every Sunday. I questioned the legitimacy of running a community school in a sectarian fashion, and I never asked my students to do what I didn't myself do. Since I was not going to accept the administration's directive I quit the school. It suddenly occurred to me that my only alternative was to build my own school. The name, Mayflower, evokes the 1620 voyage of the ship whose story I read about when I was a schoolboy. It was to be a school for all children, discriminating against none. The name, Mayflower, was our easy choice.

FI: Some would argue that the name is too Eurocentric. How would you respond?

SOLARIN: It is, indeed, Eurocentric. Nigerian society, I am inclined to say all African societies, is so steeped in religious effervescence that most people cannot do anything without dropping a nice word for the gods. In other words, it would seem secularity is a rarity in Nigeria.

FI: When was the Mayflower School founded?

SOLARIN: January 27, 1956.

FI: How many students attend the school?

SOLARIN: In 1956, seventy. In the 1991/92 school year there were 1,800 boys and girls. In 1992/93 there should be just over 1,900 boys and girls; about 1,100 boys against just over 800 girls.

FI: What makes the Mayflower School so special? And what advantages do your students have over Nigerian students who are taught in religious schools?

SOLARIN: It is special because of its secularity. We go all out to tackle the problems of life instead of spending several hours of the week explaining the significance of the deity. We have been able to debunk the conservative idea that morality is only realized from the menu of religion. We have been visited by no end of employers who openly declare they would opt for our finished products any time as compared with the products of religious schools. They are convinced our graduates work harder. And we know that, too. Our products are more sure of themselves: they are more ready to take risks. Education in self-reliance has positive results.

FI: What are some of the accomplishments of former students?

SOLARIN: We gave Nigeria its first woman engineer. When Mrs. Kasin—neé Owotomo—got to her United States university to do chemical engineering, and was asked the reason for a young country like Nigeria producing women engineers, she said she could give no more candid reason than that her high school headmaster encouraged as many girls as possible to go for engineering. Many of our students in Germany, the United Kingdom, and the United States eke out their lean incomes by working on building sites in the summer as plumbers, electricians, and tractor drivers.

20

Goodness for its Own Sake

... Dr. Tai Solarin in very many words and on many different occasions has denied the existence of God and heaven. He should be our own example of the good Samaritan. Not believing in our concept of God and heaven and thus the need for salvation, he has spent his life doing good for the selfless reason that it is good to do so. Solarin has fed the poor with food and the ignorant with knowledge. He has clothed the naked. He has suffered personal deprivations for the freedom of others....

—Adebayo Akerele in *The Guardian*,
September 5, 1992.

FI: Where does the school rank as compared to other schools? And is it a junior high school, middle school, or senior high school?

SOLARIN: It is a full high school, incorporating the junior and senior, right from its inception in 1956. There are, according to official information, 6,000 state schools in Nigeria. Here in Ogun State, where the school is located, Mayflower has been officially proclaimed the best school for the past fifteen years. There are around 500 schools in the state. Some consider Mayflower School to be one of the ten best high schools in the nation. I think I can improve on that by saying Mayflower School is one of the four best schools in the country. If the federal government would give Mayflower School a subsidy of Nl million a year instead of the N2.5 million that goes to each of what is called "unity schools" (which I have persistently called "disunity schools") Mayflower would stand a shoulder higher than any other high school in the land.

FI: How is the school run?

SOLARIN: Like any other state school—Mayflower is state owned—the state government pays for staff and equipment, but charges slightly for tuition. The Mayflower parents' organization is probably the strongest in the country. When last year the state government posted twenty-five fewer teachers into the school, the parents' organization hired the complement, built four new classrooms, and supplied desks and chairs for the students. My wife and I help to maintain the school well and the stand-by generator when the main power supply folds up, which is often.

FI: Do the teachers receive any special training?

SOLARIN: No. Because of the acute shortage of professional teachers, most of our teachers are without professional training. As long as they are good in their disciplines, they are hired as teachers to go on transmitting the knowledge the best way they can.

FI: What would it take for humanists in other African countries to build

21

schools on the Mayflower model? What qualifications, skills, and resources would be required?

SOLARIN: I think Mayflower School has been lucky not to have been stillborn. Formidable Christian churches, the Roman Catholic in particular, could have smothered it. It is alive today because its founders were convinced of what we were doing, and they were unrelenting and unsparing in their efforts. When I was in detention in Jos in 1984, a fellow detainee, a highly placed man in Jos, said that he would make sure the government paid the bill if I was ready after our release to build a Mayflower School for them. With the success of Mayflower School, I believe, today, it would take root in any other part of Nigeria, excepting strongly Muslim areas like Kano, Sokoto, and Borno states. In those places it would be tantamount to heresy to proclaim that man is the master of his fate, the captain of his soul.

What I have written above would hold for most black African countries. Tanzania and Kenya, for example, should be able to establish Mayflowers.

FI: Would you assist in such projects?

SOLARIN: I certainly would.

FI: Would it be useful to have more Mayflowers in other Nigerian cities? If so, what would be required to make this possible?

SOLARIN: The only answer to resolving most African problems is in multiplying the Mayflower School type. To get the young Africans weaned from their almost congenital reliance on fate, they must be educated to stand on their feet. The worst bane of African nondevelopment is chronic dependence on the deity to solve all earthly problems. Give everybody education for self-reliance and we will vie with the best nations everywhere. For thirty-nine years I have had all the young people that passed through my hands for years in our pre-Mayflower School days, and thirty-five years at Mayflower School—to learn this poem by William Ernest Henley:

> 1. Out of the night that covers me
> Black as the pit from pole to pole,
> I thank whatever gods may be
> For my unconquerable soul.
> 2. In the fell clutch of circumstance
> I have not winced nor cried aloud,
> Under the bludgeoning of chance,
> My head is bloody, but unbowed.
> 3. Beyond this place of wrath and tears,
> Looms but the horror of the shade,
> And yet the menace of the years,
> Finds and shall find me, unafraid.
> 4. It matters not how strait the gate

22

How charged with punishments the scroll,
I am the master of my fate,
I am the captain of my soul.

Material assistance in the nature of equipping laboratories and stocking libraries would be needed, but the first and most essential need is the leader with a sense of mission. I an not thinking of a bell-ringing pastor to loudly shout what we stand for as one who means to do plenty but says very little. I envision a Quaker sort of leader who does not shout Quakerism, but does Quakerism.

As I write this I remember that we once worked very hard harvesting a field of corn and plowing the field, spreading compost and replanting the field with corn the same day in a desperate effort not to miss the rain that seemed imminent. Had we "rested" that day, our corn would not have grown to the height it is now. Because of that effort Mayflower School is going to harvest—as we did last year—three seasons of corn as compared with the traditional two-season harvest that is typical in this part of Nigeria.

FI: How is the Mayflower School governed? Is there a board, a leadership committee, or a designated successor who could run the school in the event of your retirement?

SOLARIN: I'll answer the end of the question first. I retired sixteen years ago from the leadership of the school, surrendering it to the state. But the government realized it was a special school, so it lets me continue to assist in its further development. Individuals die but governments only succeed one another. I want us to run, as you do in America, state schools. I have quoted for the past twenty years, at least, an Irish Catholic priest who wrote: "Those who own the school own its country, own its people, own its future." And I do not want Roman Catholicism to own the future of Nigeria, just as I do not want it to be owned by Islam or Anglicanism. Nor would the religious want the school to be owned by secularism. But time will tell, for Nigeria is a secular republic, and so the future is in our favor.

My wife and I are still putting in all we can for the succor of the school, and our efforts are being appreciated. But we do own, as a private, fee-paying school, the arm that goes under the name Mayflower Junior School. Today's junior high school is younger than our Mayflower school and so the state could not ask us to jettison the name. The Mayflower Junior School has 1,300 in residence and about 300 day students. All the children's parents fight to get their children in. The state minister of education honored us with a courtesy visit five weeks ago and told us that of every five parents that visit his ministry on behalf of their children, four plead for the Mayflower School.

The school headmaster is the immediate school leader. Behind him is the Parent/Teacher's Association—a militant hard-working group. The Board of Governors, a grandiose body famous as an impotent body, lingers on. As in the case of the Parent/Teacher's Association, its members are volunteers, but because the children are not necessarily in the school they govern it is a life-less institution. The government knows I am never in sympathy with decorative establishments and does not ask questions dealing with posting of teachers, grading them, and fixing their salaries.

FI: In America, many people say, "When God was taken out of the schools, the schools went to hell." These fundamentalists charge secularism and a removal of organized prayer from the schools with the destruction of the U.S. public school system. Have similar charges ever been leveled against your school?

SOLARIN: Nigerians say, "Education without religion is like a cup of tea without sugar." I hit back by saying it is a wrong analogy. The Chinese who gave tea to the world do not drink it with sugar. I tell them that morality has nothing to do with religion. All knowledgeable Nigerians know I am not religious, but they believe I am honest. *Morals Without Religion* by Margaret Knight is one of my favorite books. All employers who have ex-Mayflower students as employees are generally surprised at the degree of honesty they see in these young Nigerians who are nurtured by the truth of humanism.

FI: Some believe that only religion can bring about wholesome family values. But your family seems to be happy and stable. What accounts for your success in this regard?

SOLARIN: I do not know of any family that is more wholesome, or happier in Nigeria, and I publicly so declare. I got married without the invitation of God's intervention; My wife was not to obey me; we are a team. Most of the marriage contracts effected around me during the past thirty years either disintegrated or are on the verge of so doing. Mine has lasted forty-one years and is still going strong. I think I owe my happy marriage to openness and dedication, no fake belief, masquerading, or cheating. Our children—the girl got married to a Roman Catholic—are both secularists. But I never have asked them questions on faith. Let them make their choices, I say.

FI: When did you become a humanist?

SOLARIN: When? At least forty years ago. Why? Because it was only during my groping for a foothold that I was happiest. I maintain great comfort and infinite happiness living as a humanist. Charles Bradlaugh, H. G. Wells, Robert Ingersoll, Jawaharlal Nehru, G. B. Shaw, and H. A. L. Fisher fused to become the rock bottom of my life today. "I shall die, as I have lived," said H. G. Wells, "the responsible centre of my world."

FI: What can humanism offer people that religion cannot? And what kinds of weaknesses can be found in religion that cannot be found in humanism?

SOLARIN: Complete faith in one's self. You are never a leaner. You are forever self-reliant. The religious man is Janus-headed. He is two in one. He professes what he doesn't believe. Nigeria is dying today of religion—outrageous religious beliefs.

FI: How many famous humanists in Nigerian history do you know of, and do you know of any who are alive today?

SOLARIN: I know of none. Even some Nigerians of my age-group whom I have known for sixty years say in my presence that I am not a humanist/atheist: that I am only being branded, being given a bad name to accelerate my hanging! Every Nigerian is born saddled with a god to worship. It took me almost thirty years to get the sledgehammer to break the shackle around my mind. It took Bertrand Russell only sixteen years and two weeks to liberate himself.

FI: How many Nigerian atheists do not wish to make their atheism known to the public?

SOLARIN: Almost 100 percent. Even where humanists feebly say so, but are not vociferous about it, families and friends would like to see them buried as religionists, just in case!

My friend Professor Ayodele Awojobi was a humanist, but he was not, like myself, a loud proclaimer of his humanism. He was buried at forty-seven, as a Christian. I am going to be the first Nigerian to be buried without prayers, church intervention, or pious priests around. I would prefer cremation but even a Mayflower graduate would not give me one! The part of my will on my disposition will be published by all Nigerian papers to leave no doubts anywhere.

FI: How is humanism treated in Nigerian media, if it is covered at all?

SOLARIN: Humanism does not have a place in our media. No one mentions atheism or humanism unless he or she is talking or writing about Tai Solarin.

FI: Throughout your life you have been heavily and courageously involved in activism. Which causes have you taken up, and what kind of resistance did you receive from government authorities?

SOLARIN: I have stood, almost exclusively, for free, universal, and compulsory education for all children, to the end of high school. More able ones would ascend with or without the springboard of parents, philanthropists, and governments. I have also stood for social justice.

Military governments everywhere in Africa react badly to criticism. The longest detention I ever had was for seventeen months (1984-1985) when I suggested that the military government then in power should not last more than three to six months.

FI: Have your atheistic views ever landed you in trouble with the government authorities?

SOLARIN: No, although I'm sure they have not gone unnoticed. Mayflower School is the only school in Nigeria where the student is not taught religion, Christian or Muslim, and does not sing or pray to the deities at the beginning or end of any day.

FI: What are some of your thoughts on the nineteenth-century freethinker Robert G. Ingersoll, and what influence did he have on your thinking?

SOLARIN: He gave me the courage to stand on my feet and declare my stand on issues where for years I was too afraid to air my doubts. He tore off the dingy curtains across my mind's eye, and let me stand, unafraid, to wend my way through life.

FI: How can humanism improve the quality of life on the African continent?

SOLARIN: It will do for every individual what it has done for me. The first great thing humanism does, I think, to humanity is to make individuals appreciate being master and captain of their fate.

FI: Do you think there should be a concerted effort to attract blacks to humanism, as is being done with African Americans for Humanism, or do you believe that humanism attracts all people for the same reasons?

SOLARIN: The former is the only way out. The Africa-based African is born in fear and shackled in fear. He has to be wakened from his apparent state of stupor or somnambulism by tossing him into the night he fears, holding aloft the light of humanism for him to see with.

FI: Why do you believe that so few Africans are humanists, and what needs to be done to make humanism better known in Nigeria? What aspects of humanism would appeal to Africans in particular?

SOLARIN: So few Africans are humanists because nonhumanists are laden with a burden that humanists have shed: fear. Most Africans are taught from birth to fear—to fear daylight, life, death. Witches, angels, the Devil or Satan, thunder, lightning, nocturnal birds are all objects that generate fear. The African child is brought up not to ask questions. Precocious children are silenced. Any human being so shackled is shorn of the equipment that is strongest in the armor of the humanist—courage. Strip the African of all objects of his fears and he will be as courageous as any other man across the world. Inject education into his or her life and you have led him or her halfway up the ladder of humanism. The most significant aspect of humanism that would, I think, appeal to the African most is the knowledge that his or her prosperity or wealth is none of the business of anybody outside himself or herself; that we can become whatever we choose to be.

My friends tell me it is God who makes me successful in my work. When I tell them I share in the responsibility of feeding, in his old age, a clergyman who preached sermons all his life, would they tell me why it was not he feeding me? They have no answer, but hold on, all the same, to their time-honored beliefs.

FI: Is it likely that humanism will ever become a popular stance in Nigeria?

SOLARIN: Yes. Humanism is not a digestible menu for the illiterate; only the educated could be humanists. Literacy in Nigeria touches only 25 percent of the people. If there is 5 percent illiteracy in America, not a single one in that percentage is a humanist. Let Nigeria climb to 60 percent literacy, and humanism will be seen marching jauntily on in colossal numbers.

But forces against broadening of the base of literacy in Nigeria are formidable. Governments in the Third World do not like the masses of the people being educated.

FI: Many blacks maintain that religion is absolutely necessary for the survival of the black community. They note that in America, for example, religious leaders like Nat Turner and Martin Luther King, Jr., used religion to unify and inspire black people to positive action. They also note that black religion has produced many black colleges and other important institutions, and that a firm belief in God actually helped many blacks through difficult times. What are your responses to these contentions?

SOLARIN: The blacks hold onto their God just as the drunken man holds on to the street lamp post—for physical support only. Habit is difficult, but not impossible to break. "The Jews hold to the hard core of national separatism, in spite of the steady evaporation of every traditional, religious justification," is the way H. G. Wells looked at the Jews. Remove the Israel/Palestine wars in the Middle East and there will be no religious rallying force among the Jews. Religion is man's childish prop.

When I was five or so, I made a journey of forty miles with my mother. To make the journey, mother gave me a "bicycle." The "bicycle" for any child of my childhood is the wheel of a bicycle which the child ran along the road. For the first fifteen miles of the journey I was way ahead of my mother. In the last stage of that journey, mother carried my "bicycle" along with our luggage, on her head. Without that "bicycle," I could never have made the journey. Today, I am able to look back to discover that I had actually carried myself and the "bicycle" as well.

FI: Many Afrocentric thinkers believe that humanism and atheism are "un-African" or possibly detrimental to the African psyche and to African unity and progress. What are your views on this?

SOLARIN: Humanism and atheism develop in the mind of man, not for a special breed of *homo Sapiens,* but for humanity, just as the wheel has been invented, not for whatever race invented it, but for humans everywhere. Whatever are branded "un-African," "for the Aryan races," are epithets for cheating.

FI: What do you believe accounts for the deep spirituality of many Africans?

SOLARIN: It is their long exposure to spirituality. Take a black African child at birth to live with the Eskimos. He would grow up completely donning the attitude of his cultural background. Nurture is mightier than nature.

FI: Many writers maintain that escalating violence between Muslims and Christians could possibly lead to another civil war in Nigeria. Is this possible?

SOLARIN: Yes. Every succeeding day aggravates the situation. And relations abroad between these two religions, or between Catholic and other denominations, succinctly points, at least for Nigeria, to the inevitability of confrontation.

FI: How influential is traditional religion—especially *juju* in Nigeria?

SOLARIN: Very influential. The more religious a person is, the more, generally, is his predisposition toward belief in *juju.*

FI: In the United States recently there have been legal cases involving videotaped actions (for example, the beating of motorist Rodney King by four Los Angeles cops). Could this kind of videotaping ever happen in Nigeria, and if not, why not?

SOLARIN: It cannot happen in Nigeria—unless it were distantly done by an operator with a powerful camera. If they noticed, the police would descend on the cameraman, destroy his camera, and, perhaps, kill him.

FI: You expressed interest in starting a humanist library. What kinds of publications would you like to include?

SOLARIN: Robert Ingersoll is so easy to read. I would want light reading materials by humanist and atheist writers. Also Bertrand Russell's *Why I Am Not a Christian;* Margaret Knight's *Worlds Without Religion;* Thomas Paine's *Age of Reason;* George Orwell's *Animal Farm*; and biographical books.

FI: Please feel free to express any final thoughts you might have on humanism, religion, and the Mayflower School.

SOLARIN: Even though I never during my twenty years as headmaster of Mayflower School sat the students down to soak them in humanism, they all knew my stand. If an expected rain fell on a Saturday, the students knew that the following Sunday morning would find us planting maize on the field instead of attending the community gathering, secular though this assembly is. I have heard chuckles from students when, occasionally, a visitor gave a word of prayer for the good work we were doing. "Lloyd George Loved my Father," later became "Awo Loved my Father" lustily sung to the tune of "Onward Christian Soldiers" by our students, to the shock of, generally, new students or visitors.

4

VIRUSES OF THE MIND

Richard Dawkins

Richard Dawkins is the Charles Simionyi Professof the Public Understanding of Science at Oxford University. He is the author of The Selfish Gene, The Blind Watchmaker, River Out of Eden, *and* Climbing Mount Improbable.

> The haven all memes depend on reaching is the human mind, but a human mind is itself an artifact created when memes restructure a human brain in order to make it a better habitat for memes. The avenues for entry and departure are modified to suit local conditions, and strengthened by various artificial devices that enhance fidelity and prolixity of replication: native Chinese minds differ dramatically from native French minds, and literate minds differ from illiterate minds. What memes provide in return to the organisms in which they reside is an incalculable store of advantages—with some Trojan horses thrown in for good measure. . . .
>
> —Daniel Dennett

Duplication-Fodder

A beautiful child close to me, six and the apple of her father's eye, believes that Thomas the Tank Engine really exists. She believes in Father Christmas, and when she grows up her ambition is to be a tooth fairy. She and her schoolfriends believe the solemn word of respected adults that tooth fairies and Father Christmas really exist. This little girl is of an age to believe whatever you tell her. If you tell her about witches changing princes into frogs she will believe you. If you tell her that bad children roast forever in hell she will have nightmares. I have just discovered that without her father's consent this sweet, trusting, gullible six-year-old is being sent, for weekly instruction, to a Roman Catholic nun. What chance has she?

A human child is shaped by evolution to soak up the culture of her people. Most obviously, she learns the essentials of their language in a matter of months. A large dictionary of words to speak, an encyclopedia of information to speak about, complicated syntactic and semantic rules to order the speaking, all are transferred from older brains into hers well before she reaches half her adult size. When you are preprogrammed to absorb useful information at a high rate, it is hard to shut out pernicious or damaging information at the same time. With so many mental mindbytes to be downloaded, so many mental codons to be duplicated, it is no wonder that child brains are gullible, open to almost any suggestion, vulnerable to subversion, easy prey to Moonies, Scientologists, and nuns. Like immune-deficient patients, children are wide open to mental infections that adults might brush off without effort.

DNA, too, includes parasitic code. Cellular machinery is extremely good at copying DNA. Where DNA is concerned it seems to have an eagerness to copy, like a child's eagerness to imitate the language of its parents. Concomitantly, DNA seems eager to be copied. The cell nucleus is a paradise of DNA, humming with sophisticated, fast, and accurate duplicating machinery.

Cellular machinery is so friendly toward DNA duplication that it is small wonder cells play host to DNA parasites; viruses, viroids, plasmids, and a riffraff of other genetic fellow travelers. Parasitic DNA even gets itself spliced seamlessly into the chromosomes themselves. "Jumping genes" are stretches of "selfish DNA" that cut or copy themselves out of chromosomes and paste themselves in elsewhere. Deadly oncogenes are almost impossible to distinguish from the legitimate genes between which they are spliced. In evolutionary time, there is probably a continual traffic from "straight" genes to "outlaw," and back again (Dawkins 1982). DNA is just DNA. The only thing that distinguishes viral DNA from host DNA is its expected method of passing in future generations. "Legitimate" host DNA is just DNA that aspires to pass into the next generation via the orthodox route of sperm or egg. "Outlaw" or parasitic DNA is just DNA that looks to a quicker, less cooperative route to the future, via a sneezed droplet or a smear of blood, rather than via a sperm or egg.

For data on a floppy disk, a computer is a humming paradise just as cell nuclei hum with eagerness to duplicate DNA. Computers and their associated disk and tape drives are designed with high fidelity in mind. As with DNA molecules, magnetized bytes don't literally "want" to be faithfully copied. Nevertheless, you can write a computer program that takes steps to duplicate itself. Not just duplicate itself within one computer, but spread itself to other computers. Computers are so good at copying bytes, and so good at faithfully obeying the instructions contained in those bytes, that they are sitting ducks to self-replicating programs: wide open to subversion by software parasites.

Any cynic familiar with the theory of selfish genes and memes would have known that modern personal computers, with their promiscuous traffic of floppy disks and e-mail links, were just asking for trouble. The only surprising thing about the current epidemic of computer viruses is that it has been so long in coming.

Computer Viruses: A Model for an Informational Epidemiology

Computer viruses are pieces of code that graft themselves into existing, legitimate programs and subvert the normal actions of those programs. They may travel on exchanged floppy disks, or over networks. They are technically distinguished from "worms" which are whole programs in their own right, usually traveling over networks. Rather different are "Trojan horses," a third category of destructive programs, which are not themselves self-replicating but rely on humans to replicate them because of their pornographic or otherwise appealing content. Both viruses and worms are programs that actually say, in computer language, "Duplicate me." Both may do other things that make their presence felt and perhaps satisfy the hole-in-corner vanity of their authors. These side effects may be "humorous" (like the virus that makes the Macintosh's built-in loudspeaker enunciate the words "Don't panic," with predictably opposite effect); malicious (like the numerous IBM viruses that erase the hard disk after a sniggering screen-announcement of the impending disaster); political (the Spanish Telecom and Beijing viruses protest about telephone costs and massacred students respectively); or simply inadvertent (the programmer is incompetent to handle the low-level system calls required to write an effective virus or worm). The famous Internet Worm, which paralyzed much of the computer power of the United States on November 2, 1988, was not intended (very) maliciously but got out of control and, within twenty-four hours, had clogged around six thousand computer memories with exponentially multiplying copies of itself.

"Memes now spread around the world at the speed of light, and replicate at rates that make even fruit flies and yeast cells look glacial in comparison. They leap promiscuously from vehicle to vehicle, and from medium to medium, and are proving to be virtually unquarantinable" (Dennett, in press). Viruses aren't limited to electronic media such as disks and data lines. On its way from one computer to another, a virus may pass through printing ink, light rays in a human lens, optic nerve impulses, and finger muscle contractions. A computer fanciers' magazine that printed the text of a virus program for the interest of its readers has been widely condemned. Indeed, such is the appeal of the virus idea to a certain kind of puerile mentality (the masculine gender is used advisedly), that publication of any kind of "how to" information on designing virus programs is rightly seen as an irresponsible act.

I am not going to publish any virus code. But there are certain tricks of effective virus design that are sufficiently well known, even obvious, that it will do no harm to mention them, as I need to do in order to develop my theme. They all stem from the virus's need to evade detection while it is spreading.

A virus that clones itself too prolifically within one computer will soon be detected because the symptoms of clogging will become too obvious to ignore. For this reason many virus programs check, before infecting a system, to make sure that they are not already on that system. Incidentally, this opens the way for a defense against viruses that is analogous to immunization. In the days before a specific antivirus program was available, I myself responded to an early infection of my own hard disk by means of a crude "vaccination." Instead of deleting the virus that I had detected, I simply disabled its coded instructions, leaving the "shell" of the virus with its characteristic external "signature" intact. In theory subsequent members of the same virus species that arrived in my system should have recognized the signature of their own kind and refrained from trying to double-infect. I don't know whether this immunization really worked, but in those days it probably was worthwhile "gutting" a virus and leaving a shell like this, rather than simply removing it lock, stock, and barrel. Nowadays it is better to hand the problem over to one of the professionally written antivirus programs.

A virus that is too virulent will be rapidly detected and scotched. A virus that instantly and catastrophically sabotages every computer in which it finds itself will not find itself in many computers. It may have a most amusing effect on one computer—erase an entire doctoral thesis or something equally side-splitting—but it won't spread as an epidemic.

Some viruses, therefore, are designed to have an effect that is small enough to be difficult to detect, but which may nevertheless be extremely damaging. There is one type that, instead of erasing disk sectors wholesale, attacks only spreadsheets, making a few random changes in the (usually financial) quantities entered in the rows and columns. Other viruses evade detection by being triggered probabilistically, for example erasing only 1 in 16 of the hard disks infected. Yet other viruses employ the time-bomb principle. Most modern computers are "aware" of the date, and viruses have been triggered to manifest themselves all around the world, on a particular date such as Friday the 13 or April Fool's Day. From the parasitic point of view, it doesn't matter how catastrophic the eventual attack is, provided the virus has had plenty of opportunity to spread first, a disturbing analogy to the Medawar/ Williams theory of aging; we are the victims of lethal and sublethal genes that mature only after we have had plenty of time to reproduce (Williams 1957). In defense, some large companies go so far as to set aside one "miner's canary" among their fleet of computers, and advance its internal calendar a week so that any time-bomb viruses will reveal themselves prematurely before the big day.

Again predictably, the epidemic of computer viruses has triggered an arms race. Antiviral software is doing a roaring trade. These antidote programs—"Interferon," "Vaccine," "Gatekeeper," and others—employ a diverse armory of tricks. Some are written with specific, known and named viruses in mind. Others intercept any attempt to meddle with sensitive systems areas of memory and warn the user.

The virus principle could in theory be used for nonmalicious, even beneficial purposes (Thimbleby 1991). Looking into the future, it is not fanciful to imagine a time when viruses, both bad and good, have become so ubiquitous that we could speak of an ecological community of viruses and legitimate programs coexisting in the silicosphere. At present, software is advertised as, say, "Compatible with System 7." In the future, products may be advertised as "Compatible with all viruses registered in the 1988 World Virus Census, immune to all listed virulent viruses, takes full advantage of the facilities offered by the following benign viruses if present. . . ." Word processing software, say, may hand over particular functions, such as word-counting and string-searches, to friendly viruses burrowing autonomously through the text.

Looking even further into the future, whole integrated software systems might grow, not by design, but by something like the growth of an ecological community such as a tropical rain forest. Gangs of mutually compatible viruses might grow up, in the same way as genomes can be regarded as gangs of mutually compatible genes (Dawkins 1982). Indeed, I have even suggested that our genomes should be regarded as gigantic colonies of viruses (Dawkins 1976). Genes cooperate with one another in genomes because natural selection has favored those genes that prosper in the presence of the other genes that happen to be common in the gene pool. Different gene pools may evolve toward different combinations of mutually compatible genes. I envisage a time when, in the same kind of way, computer viruses may evolve toward compatibility with other viruses, to form communities or gangs.

But then again, perhaps not! At any rate, I find the speculation more alarming than exciting.

At present, computer viruses don't strictly evolve. They are invented by human programmers and if they evolve they do so in the same weak sense as cars or airplanes evolve. Designers derive this year's car as a slight modification of last year's car, and they may, more or less consciously, continue a trend

34

of the last few years—further flattening of the radiator grill or whatever it may be. Computer virus designers dream up ever more devious tricks for outwitting the programmers of antivirus software. But computer viruses don't—so far—mutate and evolve by true natural section. They may do so in the future. Whether they evolve by natural selection, whether their evolution is steered by human designers, may not make much difference to their eventual performance. By either kind of evolution, we expect them to become better at concealment, and we expect them to become subtly compatible with other viruses that are at the same time prospering in the computer community.

DNA viruses and computer viruses spread for the same reason: an environment exists in which there is machinery well set up to duplicate and spread them around and to obey the instructions that the viruses embody. These two environments are, respectively, the environment of cellular physiology and the environment provided by a large community of computers and data-handling machinery. Are there are other environments like these, any other humming paradises of replication?

The Infected Mind

I have already alluded to the programmed-in gullibility a child, so useful for learning language and traditional wisdom, and so easily subverted by nuns, Moonies, and their ilk. More generally, we all exchange information with another. We don't exactly plug floppy disks into slots in one another's skulls, but we exchange sentences, both through our ears and through our eyes. We notice each other's style of moving and of dressing and are influenced. We take in advertising jingles, and are presumably persuaded by them, otherwise hardheaded businessmen would not spend so much money polluting the air with them.

Think about the two qualities that a virus, or any sort of parasitic replicator, demands of a friendly medium, the two qualities that make cellular machinery so friendly toward parasitic DNA, and that make computers so friendly toward computer viruses. These qualities are, first, a readiness to replicate information accurately, perhaps with some mistakes that are subsequently reproduced accurately; and, second, a readiness to obey instructions encoded in the information so replicated.

Cellular machinery and electronic computers excel in both these virus-friendly qualities. How do human brains match up? As faithful duplicators they are certainly less perfect than either cells or electronic computers. Nevertheless, they are still pretty good, perhaps about as faithful as an RNA virus through not as good as DNA with all its elaborate proofreading measures against textual degradation. Evidence of the fidelity of brains, especially child brains, as data duplicators is provided by language itself. Shaw's Professor Higgins was able by ear alone to place Londoners in the street where they grew up. Fiction is not evidence for anything, but everyone knows that Higgins's fictional skill is only an exaggeration of something we can all do. Any American can tell Deep South from Midwest, New England from Hillbilly. Any New Yorker can tell Bronx from Brooklyn. Equivalent claims could be substantiated for any country. What this phenomenon means is that human brains are capable of pretty accurate copying (otherwise the accents of, say, Newcastle would not be stable enough to be recognized) but with some mistakes (otherwise pronunciation would not evolve, and all speakers of a language would inherit identically the same accents from their remote ancestors). Language evolves, because it has the great stability and the slight changeability that are prerequisites for any evolving system.

The second requirement of a virus-friendly environment—that it should obey a program of coded instructions—is again only quantitatively less true for brains than for cells or computers. We sometimes obey orders from one another, but also we sometimes don't. Nevertheless, it is a telling fact that, the world over, the vast majority of children follow the religion of their parents rather than any of the other available religions. Instructions to genuflect, to bow toward Mecca, to nod one's head rhythmically toward the wall, to shake like a maniac, to "speak in tongues"—the list of such arbitrary and pointless motor patterns offered by religion alone is extensive—are obeyed, if not slavishly, at least with some reasonably high statistical probability.

Less portentously, and again especially prominent in children, the "craze" is a striking example of behavior that owes more to epidemiology than to rational choice. Yo-yos, hula hoops, and pogo sticks, with their associated behavior fixed patterns, sweep through schools, and more sporadically leap from school to school, in ways that differ from a measles epidemic in no serious particular. Ten years ago, you could have traveled thousands of miles through the United States and never seen a baseball cap turned back to front. Today the reverse baseball cap is ubiquitous. I do not know what the pattern of geographic spread of the reverse baseball cap was precisely, but epidemiology is certainly among the professions primarily qualified to study it. We don't have to get into arguments about "determinism"; we don't have to claim that children are compelled to imitate their fellows' hat fashions. It is enough that their hat-wearing behavior, as a matter of fact, is statistically affected by the hat-wearing behavior of their fellows.

Trivial though they are, crazes provide us with yet more circumstantial evidence that human minds, especially perhaps juvenile ones, have the qualities that we have singled out as desirable for an informational parasite. At the very least the mind is a plausible candidate for infection by something like a computer virus, even if it is not quite such a parasite's dream-environment as a cell nucleus or an electronic computer.

It is intriguing to wonder what it might be like, from the inside, if one's mind were the victim of a "virus." This might be a deliberately designed parasite, like a present-day computer virus. Or it might be an inadvertently mutated and unconsciously evolved parasite. Either way, especially if the evolved parasite was the memic descendant of a long line of successful ancestors, we are entitled to expect the typical "mind virus" to be pretty good at its job of getting itself successfully replicated.

Progressive evolution of more effective mind-parasites will have two aspects. New "mutants" (either random or designed by humans) that are better at spreading will become more numerous. And there will be a ganging up of ideas that flourish in one another's presence, ideas that mutually support one another just as genes do and as I have speculated computer viruses may do one day. We expect that replicators will go around together from brain to brain in mutually compatible gangs. These gangs will come to constitute a package, which may be sufficiently stable to deserve a collective name such as Roman Catholicism or Voodoo. It doesn't too much matter whether we analogize the whole package to a single virus, or each one of the component parts to a single virus. The analogy is not that precise anyway, just as the distinction between a computer virus and a computer worm is nothing to get worked up about. What matters is that minds are friendly environments to parasitic, self-replicating ideas or information, and that minds are typically massively infected.

Like computer viruses, successful mind viruses will tend to be hard for their victims to detect. If you are the victim of one, the chances are that you won't know it, and may even vigorously deny it. Accepting that a virus might be difficult to detect in your own mind, what telltale signs might you look out for? I shall answer by imagining how a medical textbook might describe the typical symptoms of a sufferer (arbitrarily assumed to be male).

1. The patient typically finds himself impelled by some deep, inner conviction that something is true, or right, or virtuous: a conviction that doesn't seem to owe anything to evidence or reason, but which, nevertheless, he feels as totally compelling and convincing. We doctors refer to such a belief as "faith."

2. Patients typically make a positive virtue of faith's being strong and unshakable, in spite of not being based upon evidence. Indeed, they may feel that the less evidence there is, the more virtuous the belief (see below).

This paradoxical idea that lack of evidence is a positive virtue where faith is concerned has something of the quality of a program that is self-sustaining, because it is self-referential (see the chapter "On Viral Sentences and Self-Replicating Structures" in Hofstadter 1985). Once the proposition is believed, it automatically undermines opposition to itself. The "lack of evidence is a virtue" idea would be an admirable sidekick, ganging up with faith itself in a clique of mutually supportive viral programs.

3. A related symptom, which a faith-sufferer may also present, is the conviction that "mystery," per se, is a good thing. It is not a virtue to solve mysteries. Rather we should enjoy them, even revel in their insolubility.

Any impulse to solve mysteries could be seriously inimical to the spread of a mind virus. It would not, therefore, be surprising if the idea that "mysteries are better not solved" was a favored member of a mutually supporting gang of viruses. Take the "Mystery of the Transubstantiation." It is easy and nonmysterious to believe that in some symbolic or metaphorical sense the eucharistic wine turns into the blood of Christ. The Roman Catholic doctrine of transubstantiation, however, claims far more. The "whole substance" of the wine is converted into the blood of Christ; the appearance of wine that remains is "merely accidental," "inhering in no substance" (Kenny 1986 p. 72). Transubstantiation is colloquially taught as meaning that the wine "literally" turns into the blood of Christ. Whether in its obfuscatory Aristotelian or its franker colloquial form, the claim of transubstantiation can be made only if we do serious violence to the normal meanings of words like *substance* and *literally*. Redefining words is not a sin, but, if we use words like *whole substance* and *literally* for this case, what word are we going to use when we really and truly want to say that something did actually happen? As Anthony Kenny observed of his own puzzlement as a young seminarian, "For all I could tell, my typewriter might be Benjamin Disraeli transubstantiated. . . ."

Roman Catholics whose belief in infallible authority compels them to accept that wine becomes physically transformed into blood despite all appearances refer to the "mystery" of the transubstantiation. Calling it a mystery makes everything O.K., you see. At least, it works for a mind well prepared by background infection. Exactly the same trick is performed in the "mystery" of the Trinity. Mysteries are not meant to be solved, they are meant to strike awe. The "mystery is a virtue" idea comes to the aid of the Catholic, who would otherwise find intolerable the obligation to believe the obvious nonsense of the transubstantiation and the "three-in-one." Again, the belief that "mystery is a virtue" has a self-referential ring. As Hofstadter might put it, the very mysteriousness of the belief moves the believer to perpetuate the mystery.

An extreme symptom of "mystery is a virtue" infection is Tertullian's *"Certum est quia impossibile est"* (It is certain because it is impossible). That way madness lies. One is tempted to quote Lewis Carroll's White Queen, who, in response to Alice's "One can't believe impossible things," retorted, "I daresay you haven't had much practice. . . . When I was your age, I always did it for half-an-hour a day. Why, sometimes I believed as many as six impossible things before breakfast." Or Douglas Adams's Electric Monk, a labor-saving device programmed to do your believing for you, which was capable of "believing things they'd have difficulty believing in Salt Lake City" and which, at the moment of being introduced to the reader, believed, contrary to all evidence, that everything in the world was a uniform shade of pink. But White Queens and Electric Monks become less funny when you realize that these virtuoso believers are indistinguishable from revered theologians in real life. "It is by all means to be believed, because it is absurd" (Tertullian again). Sir Thomas Browne quotes Tertullian with approval, and goes further: "Methinks there be not impossibilities enough in religion for an active faith." And "I desire to exercise my faith in the difficultest point: for to credit ordinary and visible objects is not faith, but persuasion."

I have the feeling that something more interesting is going on here than just plain insanity or surrealist nonsense, something akin to the admiration we feel when we watch a ten-ball juggler on a tightrope. It is as though the faithful gain prestige through managing to believe even more ridiculous things than their rivals succeed in believing. Are these people testing—exercising—their believing muscles, training themselves to believe impossible things so that they can take in their stride the merely improbable things that they are ordinarily called upon to believe?

While I was writing this, the *Guardian* (July 29, 1991) fortuitously carried a beautiful example. It came in an interview with a rabbi undertaking the bizarre task of vetting the kosher-purity of food products right back to the ultimate origin of their minutest ingredients. He was currently agonizing over whether to go all the way to China to scrutinize the menthol that goes into cough sweets. "Have you ever tried checking Chinese menthol . . . it was extremely difficult, especially since the first letter we sent received the reply in best Chinese English, 'The product contains no kosher. . . .' China has only recently started opening up to kosher investigators. The methol should be OK, but you can never be absolutely sure unless you visit." These kosher investigators run a telephone hotline on which up-to-the-minute red-alerts of suspicion are recorded against chocolate bars and cod-liver oil. The rabbi sighs that the green-inspired trend away from artificial colors and flavors "makes life miserable in the kosher field because you have to follow all these things back." When the interviewer asks him why he bothers with this obviously pointless exercise, he makes it very clear that the point is precisely that there is no point:

> That most of the Kashrut laws are divine ordinances without reason given is 100 per cent the point. It is very very easy not to murder people. Very easy. It is a little bit harder not to steal because one is tempted occasionally. So that is no great proof that I believe in God or am fulfilling His will. But, if He tells me not to have a cup of coffee with milk in it with my mincemeat and peas at lunchtime, that is a test. The only reason I am doing that is because I have been told to do so. It is doing something difficult.

Helena Cronin has suggested to me that there may be an analogy here to Zahavi's handicap theory of sexual selection and the evolution of signals (Zahavi 1975). Long unfashionable, even ridiculed (Dawkins 1976), Zahavi's theory has been recently rehabilitated (Grafen 1990a, b) and is now taken seriously by evolutionary biologists (Dawkins 1989). Zahavi suggests that peacocks, for instance, evolve their absurdly burdensome fans with their ridiculously conspicuous (to predators) colors, precisely because they are burdensome and dangerous, and therefore impressive to females. The peacock is, in effect, saying: "Look how fit and strong I must be, since I can afford to carry around this preposterous tail."

To avoid misunderstanding of the subjective language in which Zahavi likes to make his points, I should add that the biologist's convention of personifying the unconscious actions of natural selection is taken for granted here. Grafen has translated the argument into an orthodox Darwinian mathematical model, and it works. No claim is here being made about the intentionality or awareness of peacocks and peahens. They can be as sphexish or as intentional as you please (Dennett 1983, 1984). Moreover, Zahavi's theory is general enough not to depend upon a Darwinian underpinning. A flower advertising its nectar to a "skeptical" bee could benefit from the Zahavi principle. But so could a human salesman seeking to impress a client.

The premise of Zahavi's idea is that natural selection will favor skepticism among females (or among recipients of advertising messages generally). The only way for a male (or any advertiser) to authenticate his boast of strength (quality, or whatever it is) is to prove that it is true by shouldering a truly costly handicap—a handicap *that only a genuinely strong* (high quality, etc.) male could bear. It may be called the "principle of costly authentication." And now to the point. Is it possible that some religious doctrines are favored not *in spite of* being ridiculous but precisely *because* they are ridiculous? Any wimp in religion could believe that bread symbolically represents the body of Christ, but it takes a real red-blooded Catholic to believe something as daft as the transubstantiation. If you can believe that, you can believe anything, and (witness the story of Doubting Thomas) these people are trained to see that as a virtue.

Let us return to our list of symptoms that someone afflicted with the mental virus of faith, and its accompanying gang of secondary infections, may expect to experience.

4. The sufferer may find himself behaving intolerantly toward vectors of rival faiths, in extreme cases even killing them or advocating their deaths. He may be similarly violent in his disposition toward apostates (people who once held the faith but have renounced it); or toward heretics (people who espouse a different—often, perhaps significantly, only very slightly different—version of the faith). He may also feel hostile toward other modes of thought that are potentially inimical to his faith, such as the method of scientific reason that may function rather like a piece of antiviral software.

The threat to kill the distinguished novelist Salman Rushdie is only the latest in a long line of sad examples. On the very same day that I wrote this, the Japanese translator of *The Satanic Verses* was found murdered, a week after a near-fatal attack on the Italian translator of the same book. By the way, the apparently opposite symptom of "sympathy" for Muslim "hurt," voiced by by the Archbishop of Canterbury and other Christian leaders (verging, in the case of the Vatican, on outright criminal complicity) is, of course, a manifestation of the symptom we diagnosed earlier: the delusion that faith, however obnoxious its results, has to be respected simply because it is faith.

Murder is an extreme, of course. But there is an even more extreme symptom, and that is suicide in the militant service of a faith. Like a soldier ant programmed to sacrifice her life for germ-line copies of the genes that did the programming, a young Arab or Japanese is taught that to die in a holy war is the quickest way to heaven. Whether the leaders who exploit him really believe this does not diminish the brutal power that the "suicide mission virus" wields on behalf of the faith. Of course suicide, like murder, is a mixed blessing: would-be converts may be repelled, or may treat with contempt a faith that is perceived as insecure enough to need such tactics.

More obviously, if too many individuals sacrifice themselves the supply of believers could run low. This was true of a notorious example of faith-inspired suicide, though in this case it was not "kamikaze" death in battle. The Peoples' Temple sect went extinct when its leader, the Reverend Jim Jones, led the bulk of his followers from the United States to the Promised Land of "Jonestown" in the Guyana jungle where he persuaded more than nine hundred of them, children first, to drink cyanide. The macabre affair

41

was fully investigated by a team from the San Francisco *Chronicle* (Kilduff and Javers 1978).

> Jones, "the Father," had called his flock together and told them it was time to depart for heaven.
> "We're going to meet," he promised, "in another place."
> The words kept coming over the camp's loudspeakers.
> "There is great dignity in dying. It is a great demonstration for everyone to die."

Incidentally, it does not escape the trained mind of the alert sociobiologist that Jones, within his sect in earlier days "proclaimed himself the only person permitted to have sex" (presumably his partners were also permitted). A secretary would arrange for Jones's liaisons. She would call up and say, "Father hates to do this, but he has this tremendous urge and could you please. . . ?" His victims were not only female. One seventeen-year-old male follower, from the days when Jones's community was still in San Francisco, told how he was taken for dirty weekends to a hotel where Jones received a "minister's discount for Rev. Jim Jones and son." The same boy said:

> I was really in awe of him. He was more than a father. I would have killed my parents for him.

What is remarkable about the Reverend Jim Jones is not his own self-serving behavior but the almost superhuman gullibility of his followers. Given such prodigious credulity, can anyone doubt that human minds are ripe for malignant infection?

Admittedly, the Reverend Jones conned only a few thousand people. But his case is an extreme, the tip of the iceberg. The same eagerness to be conned by religious leaders is widespread. Most of us would have been prepared to bet that nobody could get away with going on television and saying, in all but so many words, "Send me your money, so that I can use it to persuade other suckers to send me their money too." Yet today, in every major city in the United States, you can find at least one television evangelist channel entirely devoted to this transparent confidence trick. And they get away with it in sackfuls. Faced with suckerdom on this awesome scale, it is hard not to feel a grudging sympathy with the shiny-suited conmen. Until you realize that not all the suckers are rich, and that it is often widows' mites on which the evangelists are growing fat. I have even heard one of them explicitly invoking the principle that I now identify with Zahavi's principle of costly authentication. God really appreciates a donation, he said with passionate sincerity, only when that donation is so large that it hurts. Elderly paupers were literally wheeled on to testify how much happier they felt since they had made over their little all to the reverend whoever it was.

5. The patient may notice that the particular convictions that he holds, while having nothing to do with evidence, do seem to owe a great deal to epidemiology. Why, he may wonder, do I hold this set of convictions rather than that set? Is it because I surveyed all the world's faiths and chose the one whose claims seemed most convincing? Almost certainly not. If you have a faith, it is statistically overwhelmingly likely that it is the same faith as your parents and grandparents had. No doubt soaring cathedrals, stirring music, moving stories, and parables help a bit. But by far the most important variable determining your religion is the accident of birth. The convictions that you so passionately believe would have been a completely different, and largely contradictory, set of convictions, if only you had happened to be born in a different place. Epidemiology, not evidence.

6. If the patient is one of the rare exceptions who follows a different religion from his parents, the explanation may still be epidemiological. To be sure, it is possible that he dispassionately surveyed the world's faiths and chose the most convincing one. But it is statistically more probable that he has been exposed to a particularly potent infective agent—a John Wesley, a Jim Jones, or a St. Paul. Here we are talking about horizontal transmission, as in measles. Before, epidemiology was that of vertical transmission, as in Huntington's Chorea.

7. The internal sensations of the patient may be startlingly reminiscent of those more ordinarily associated with sexual love. This is an extremely potent force in the brain, and is not surprising that some viruses have evolved to exploit it. St. Teresa of Avila's famously orgasmic vision is too notorious to need quoting again. More seriously, and on a less crudely sensual plane, the philosopher Anthony Kenny provides moving testimony to the pure delight that awaits those that manage to believe in the mystery of transubstantiation. After describing his ordination as a Roman Catholic priest, empowered by laying on of hands to celebrate Mass, he goes on that he vividly recalls:

> . . . the exaltation of the first months during which I had the power to say Mass. Normally a slow and sluggish riser, I would leap early out of bed, fully awake and full of excitement at the thought of the momentous act I was privileged to perform. I rarely said the public Community Mass: most days I celebrated alone at a side altar with a junior member of the College to serve as acolyte and congregation. But that made no difference to the solemnity of the sacrifice or the validity of the consecration.
>
> It was touching the body of Christ, the closeness of the priest to Jesus, which most enthralled me. I would gaze on the Host after the words of consecration, soft-eyed like a lover looking into the eyes of his beloved. . . . Those early days as a

priest remain in my memory as days of fulfillment and tremulous happiness; something precious, and yet too fragile to last, like a romantic love-affair brought up short by the reality of an ill-assorted marriage. (Kenny 1986, pp. 101 102)

Dr. Kenny is affectingly believable that it felt to him, a young priest, as though he was in love with the consecrated host. What a brilliantly successful virus! On the same page, incidentally, Kenny also shows us that the virus is transmitted contagiously—if not literally then at least in some sense—from the palm of the infecting bishop's hand through the top of the new priest's head: "If Catholic doctrine is true, every priest validly ordained derives his orders in an unbroken line of laying on of hands, through the bishop who ordained him, back to one of the twelve Apostles . . . there must be centuries-long, recorded chains of layings on of hands. It surprises me that priests never seem to trouble to trace their spiritual ancestry in this way, finding out who ordained their bishop, and who ordained him, and so on to Julius II, or Celestine V or Hildebrand, or Gregory the Great, perhaps" (Kenny 1986 p. 101). It surprises me, too.

Is Science a Virus?

No. Not unless all computer programs are viruses. Good useful programs spread because people evaluate them, recommend them, and pass them on. Computer viruses spread solely because they embody the coded instruction: "Spread me." Scientific ideas, like all memes, are subject to a kind of natural selection, and this might look superficially viruslike. But the selective forces that scrutinize scientific ideas are not arbitrary or capricious. They are exacting, well-honed rules, and they do not favor pointless self-serving behavior. They favor all the virtues laid out in textbooks of standard methodology: testability, evidential support, precision, quantifiability, consistency, intersubjectivity, repeatability, universality, progressiveness, independence of cultural milieu, and so on. Faith spreads despite a total lack of every single one of these virtues.

You may find elements of epidemiology in the spread of scientific ideas, but it will be largely descriptive epidemiology. The rapid spread of a good idea through the scientific community may even look like a description of a measles epidemic. But when you examine the underlying reasons you find that they are good ones, satisfying the demanding standards of scientific method. In the history of the spread of faith you will find little else but epidemiology, and causal epidemiology at that. The reason why person A believes one thing and B believes another is simply and solely that A was born on one continent and B on another. Testability, evidential support, and the rest aren't even remotely considered. For scientific belief, epidemiology merely comes along afterward and describes the history of its acceptance. For religious belief, epidemiology is the root cause.

Epilogue: Happily, Viruses Don't Win Every Time

Many children emerge unscathed from the worst that nuns and mullahs can throw at them. Anthony Kenny's own story has a happy ending. He eventually renounced his orders because he could no longer tolerate the obvious contradictions within Catholic belief, and he is now a highly respected scholar. But one cannot help remarking that it must be a powerful infection indeed that took a man of his wisdom and intelligence—now president of the British Academy, no less—three decades to fight off. Am I unduly alarmist to fear for the soul of my six-year-old innocent?

References

Browne, Sir T. 1635. *Religio Medici I,* 9, p. 11.
Dawkins, R. 1976. *The Selfish Gene.* Oxford: Oxford University Press.
————. 1982. *The Extended Phenotype.* Oxford: W. H. Freeman.
————. 1989. *The Selfish Gene.* Second Edition. Oxford: Oxford University Press.
Dennett, D. C. 1983. Intentional systems in cognitive ethology: The "Panglossian paradigm" defended. *Behavioral and Brain Sciences.* 6, 343–390.
————. 1984. *Elbow Room: The Varieties of Free Will Worth Wanting.* Oxford: Oxford University Press.
Grafen, A. 1990a. Sexual selection unhandicapped by the Fisher process. *Journal of Theoretical Biology,* 144, 473–516.
————. 1990b. Biological signals as handicaps. *Journal of Theoretical Biology,* 144, 517–546.
Hofstadter, D. R. 1985. *Metamagical Themas.* Harmondsworth: Penguin.
Kenny, A. 1986. *A Path from Rome.* Oxford: Oxford University Press.
Kilduff, M., and R. Javers. 1978. *The Suicide Cult.* New York: Bantam.
Thimbleby. H. 1991. Can viruses ever be useful? *Computers and Security,* 10, 111–114.
Williams, G. C. 1957 Pleiotropy, natural selection, and the evolution of senescence. *Evolution,* 11, 398–411.
Zahavi, A. 1975. Mate selection—a selection for a handicap. *Journal of Theoretical Biology,* 53, 205–214.

This is an abridged version of an article originally commissioned for B. Dahlbom, editor of Dennett and His Critics: Demystifying Mind *(Oxford: Blackwell, in press, 1993). It was also delivered as the 1992 Voltaire Lecture, sponsored by the British Humanist Association, and as the keynote address of the 1992 conference of the Committee for the Scientific Investigation of Claims of the Paranormal.*

45

5

DO CHILDREN NEED RELIGION?
AN INTERVIEW WITH MARTHA FAY

Martha Fay, author of A Mortal Condition, *has written for the* New York Times Magazine, Time, *and* Life, *among other publications.* When Do Children Need Religion? *was published in 1993, it received considerable attention, including feature articles in major dailies like the* Los Angeles Times *and the* New York Times. *Clearly the book had struck a nerve among a generation of parents who, as Fay says in her introduction, find themselves "surprised and somewhat bewildered by the sudden urgency of a question that had completely failed to attract their interest previously: Do children need religion?—or more pertinently: Does my child need religion?" She adds, "And of course, ready or not, the questions will come. For parents contemplating the choices before them, they are but the beginning."*

Fay answers questions with questions, those of the parents she interviewed, and some of her own. Here, she shares a few of the answers they found.

—Molleen Matsumura
FI Associate Editor

FREE INQUIRY: I'd like to begin with a somewhat personal question. The title of your book might lead readers to think that they'll find some kind of definitive answer, but in fact it's more like a discussion with you as the moderator, making sure that many aspects of the question are explored, and many voices are heard. At the end, describing your conversation with your daughter and another child in an Italian chapel, you sound almost ambivalent. Did you reach a conclusion?

MARTHA FAY: At the time I felt reassured by that conversation. I had come to terms with my questions. I do feel that my child and many other children live outside any particular cultural tradition. I feel that by the choice I have made I have removed her from the tradition I was raised in, though of course, that tradition is itself changing. I think the only solution, for anybody, is the honest one, the one that conveys your own sense of conviction. I include in that the fact that there will always be a certain ambivalence. I'm not an absolutist, but, as someone who was raised a Catholic, I can't help but bring my own scrupulosity to these questions. I would not advise other people what to do, and of course I have second thoughts, but I find I am more comfortable casting my lot not with my own small group, but with humanity at large. Living outside a religious framework is, for many people, more than they can stand. For many people religion is a necessary crutch, and they're willing to look the other way when it comes to the small details they might not agree with. Reality straight is more than they can take. It does suit me, but it is difficult.

I came to the positions I hold in my late twenties, with a better-than-average education in theology, but what I was asking in the book is, does one charge right in to address these big questions with one's children? The way in which adults have developed and come to hold their beliefs is often very different from the way they present those beliefs to their children.

FI: Your book centers on conversations with parents. Did you also learn something from their children? Some of the children brought up without religion seemed quite comfortable with that. How about the ones who were given some kind of religious training even though their parents were non-believers?

FAY: I didn't interview many children, I concentrated on adults, and in fact, as I worked on the book, I told people I was writing a book about religious ambivalence. The adults I spoke with kept returning to their own recollections, and I had to keep steering them back to conversations about their children. I only came across one person who was not a believer yet sent his children to Sunday school. It was more often the case that people who had a tentative belief in God, or who were uncertain about what they thought, were the ones who sent their children to Sunday school, rather than clear atheists.

We live in a culture where God and references to a deity are ubiquitous, and many people just aren't able to let go of religion. They don't have another ice floe to jump to.

FI: You quoted a study, "The Beliefs and Moral Values of America's Children," that suggested that Sunday school has little or no effect on children's moral judgment. Did your interviews with parents and religious educators give you a different impression?

FAY: That happened to be a very interesting but inconclusive study, in which many sections seemed to contradict each other, and children's positions were splintered. It was *my* interpretation that the apparent positive effect of Sunday school attendance may really have reflected the attitudes of parents who were very caring and involved in their children's moral development.

Many parents I interviewed simply felt unable to go it alone. But parents also found they couldn't just send their children off to Sunday school and expect that to be the whole solution. And I found that many churches had been telling parents that they shouldn't expect their kids to go to Sunday school unless they were willing to attend the church themselves.

A sidebar to this is something that has been an issue in the Catholic church for years. Traditionally, parents who wanted their kids baptized in the Catholic church were practicing Catholics themselves. But with a decrease in attendance or formal compliance among Catholics there was an increase in the number of nominal Catholics who wanted their children baptized for the sake of tradition alone, the way they do in Europe, because it's part of the culture. But the church has said no, that it would not baptize children if the parents weren't going to be involved. And this is a great ongoing row, because the church is saying if you're not going to raise your children Catholic, don't have them baptized, it's inappropriate, it's hypocritical. Whereas the ex-Catholics, or nonreligious Catholics, say, "It's a culture as well, and I want to participate in it, and how can you deny me this?" And of course I can see both points of view. Whatever their belief systems, churches are communities, and they're entitled to demand, or at least ask, something of their participants.

FI: That goes to the question that your book explores—not whether children need religion so much as whether parents need the help of religious institutions and beliefs in raising their children. I was especially struck by your quoting a family therapist who said that sometimes nonreligious parents invoked his authority. Was that need for an external authority a major factor in some parents' reliance on religion?

FAY: Among people who were regular churchgoers, there was a strong sense that there was a need for support. Not necessarily a substitute authority, but reinforcement for their position. They often felt that in the schools, and elsewhere in the country, there were not many moral voices being raised. The difference between finding reinforcement and relying on external authority tends to blur in people's minds, and there are people who actually wish they could believe and wish they could invoke some external authority.

I think this is connected with the popularity of books offering advice about child-rearing. People turn to books because they don't trust themselves.

FI: Many of the parents who felt some nostalgia for their religious up-bringings, or even a need to repeat some aspects, seemed more interested in ritual and emotion than theology. They talked about loving the smell of incense, or the enjoyment of singing hymns. Others specifically said they dislike the emotional appeal of ritual. What's your view on this issue?

FAY: Theology turned out to be the subject that was least discussed. Most people were simply uninterested in theological questions, and in fact many, though not all, had had no theological education. For the most part, it was Catholics who had received the most extensive theological education, but even for them theology was a secondary issue.

What was apparent was that, while we live in a secular age, most people aren't ready for it emotionally, just as they aren't ready for the issues raised by such scientific breakthroughs as test-tube babies or genetic testing, and the many sticky questions they create. Religions have always offered ways to explain things, and as much as anything, I think it's these explanations that people miss. I think this explains the popularity of beliefs in UFOs, the imagery of alien abduction, and so on. Such things help people make sense out of confusion. You know, some people who adhere to what seem to be truly bizarre theologies lead very conventional daily lives, and have beautifully behaved children.

FI: How did differences in parents' backgrounds affect their decisions? I would imagine conversations got really interesting when one parent was religious and the other a freethinker. And how did children feel about these differences?

FAY: When parents are quarreling, kids are miserable. Several adults had terrible memories of the times their parents of different denominations got into power struggles, and these people wanted nothing to do with religion. They were angry about what had happened to them, and in most cases chose not to provide their children with a religious experience of any kind.

On the other hand, I didn't come across many families in which parents were at war over their children's souls. What did happen was that people decided that their personal lives were more important than the choice of a particular religion. People are less willing to cede to religion what earlier generations did. And though most of the people I spoke to insisted that they were believers and that faith made a difference to them, in terms of observable conduct, people with and without faith are often indistinguishable.

FI: You mentioned one nonbelieving mother who commented that her daughter got angry when she denied the existence of God. The little girl must have gotten that idea from outside the home. How much were parents who brought in religion responding to social pressure?

FAY: I would say that it's not so much a question of giving in to social pressure as acceding to social convention in the sense that few parents felt the need to combat every reference to God when their kids were young. I drew a variety of responses on this issue, but most people were very comfortable with the idea that their kids would think for a time that God existed.

FI: One of the issues you raise is that Judeo-Christian values, and biblical literary imagery, are an important part of our cultural history, and at one point, for example, you asked whether there is any image that better communicates the preciousness of children than the story of the infant Jesus. Not to me! That story wasn't part of my childhood. But I've always loved to read myths of various cultures, and I immediately thought of the story of Ceres and Persephone. Later, you commented that many people no longer identify themselves by their religion, saying, "I'm a Baptist," or "I'm a Catholic." And if they did, now they might say they're Muslim or Buddhist. Maybe the change away from a common Judeo-Christian culture has gone farther than anybody thinks, and we'll have to find other ways to connect children with society at large.

FAY: That's a very good point. You made me think of a woman I know, an atheist, who when her son died at the age of seven, told the story of Persephone at his memorial ceremony. But most people aren't classicists, and that tradition isn't available to them, either.

Yet we do need ways to extend the feelings in these stories to children. Feelings of safety, preciousness, and connection. We haven't been doing this well, and a way has to be found. Maybe Joseph Campbell was right when he said that we need a new mythology, though the one he proposed, a sort of space mythology, is not what I would have chosen. We're bereft several times over; people are no longer familiar with either Greek or Judeo-Christian mythology. But the problem with Campbell's suggestion is you can't just declare new myths. They evolve—like the Kennedy myth. The New Agers who believe in such things as reincarnation are grasping for myths, too.

What I do is use literature. I don't have a scheme, but I have read the Greek myths to my daughter, and now she's reading myths from other cultures. We talk about everything we read.

FI: What was most interesting for you about working on the book?

FAY: Simply writing the book was immensely interesting intellectually—the reading it entailed, and thinking and talking to people. What was rewarding wasn't a single discovery, but the whole process of delving into the most interesting questions that most of us think about. The focus on children gave it a particular tilt, but most of the time I was really talking with people about their own peace of mind. In thinking about their children, they faced the problems stemming from our own childhoods that we still have as adults.

FI: Was there material from your research that you wish you could have included in the book but were unable to?

FAY: What I regret having to omit is not an area of traditional concern, like having left out, say, ethics, so much as how I was taken by people's private stories of a religious or nonreligious past, and how closely interwoven that perspective is with people's personal histories. They all become artifacts of their past. For example, the "saints" of the red diaper babies—the people they heard about in socialist summer camps—were people like Paul Robeson and Sacco and Vanzetti. I did try to touch on that in the chapter on identity— how interwoven religion or its substitutes are with the texture of people's personal pasts. They bring these ideas into their adult lives, and when they no longer believe, they don't quite know what to do with all those remnants.

We're all products of our parents, whatever our religious background. Whatever people's current belief systems, their histories and their habits of speech, thought, and celebration come out of that past. In my apartment, for example, it looks like I'm still a Catholic; I have a Christmas tree, and certain kinds of religious art, like Mexican shrines and Italian holy water fonts. I grew up with these things, and what I own now is not all kitsch—some of it is quite beautiful. I didn't grow up on Buddhist prayer wheels! So, that's part of my culture, just as anyone who grew up in a Lutheran church grew up with Bach.

I became aware while working on the book of how deeply religion was embedded in people's pasts. They recalled Methodist hymns, or chapel at boarding school, or Baptist rallies in the summer in the South. Most everyone had some such memory, and when they abandoned the belief system that went with it, they found it hard to know what to do with the memory. It's one thing to be a fiction writer, and to try to make use of it in a story, but most people don't have any place to take that part of their lives. It was sad and touching, and I wish I could have written about some of the families in profile and been able to capture that. Because these histories have a lot to do with the way people see themselves and the way they act in the world; even if their belief systems are no longer powerful, their habits of community, their habits of looking at things, and their habits of conversation are still powerful—even such things as whether they like to sing in public or don't. Because of the organization of the book, I couldn't fully convey that power of religion and how it affects people. It's one of the reasons people find it so difficult to let go.

FI: Your sympathy is very evident in the book. It was there even when you disagreed with people, wasn't it?

FAY: Recently I was talking to a friend, somebody I'd mentioned in the book, and he said he wondered whether I should have come down more strongly against religion and made it more controversial. He was half joking; he didn't mean only for the sake of getting the book more attention, but also in terms of what I really believe. And I said that you could make a good argument that maybe I should have been tougher, more anti-religious, or conveyed my own position more strongly—but the fact is that I did feel such tremendous sympathy for people when I was writing it, and especially for their difficulty letting go of the past.

And yes, this was true even when I felt a lot of disagreement with their belief systems. In terms of actual things one believes to be true or good, there was very little difference except that I don't base my belief in God, and someone else does. That was true with two of my sisters. We don't have many arguments about what ought to be, or how people ought to behave. It's just that they happen to locate their beliefs in a God, who's some remnant of the traditional God, and I don't. I think that that's one of the interesting things about where we are now. That people who locate their belief, or anchor it, in different things, may agree in important ways, while often people who appear to anchor their beliefs in the "same" God are more quarrelsome than those of us who are on "opposite" sides.

FI: It seems the book gave you a lot of insight into what people go through in making the decision on whether their children need religion. How would you advise people on the issue, for example, on whether they should send their kids to Sunday school?

FAY: What I can say from both my own experience and that of the people I interviewed is that you can pass on your beliefs successfully. It's not a guarantee, but you can. The problem—for some of us anyway—is that of coming to terms with the relative grimness in this culture, and the relative difficulty of finding support for the beliefs you do have. That's what the book is about, that it's harder to answer your child's questions outside the context of a belief system with a God who's going to rescue you, and outside a social consensus.

I don't have any specific advice, except that what was very clear to me, from talking to people about it and thinking about it myself, over and over again, is that it's pointless to do anything you don't believe in. Not only as a matter of honesty, but also there's a moral and psychological absurdity to it. It seems to me that sending your child to a Sunday school in a denomination where you wouldn't feel comfortable would be a very strange thing to do. If you had a choice, you wouldn't send your child to a school where you disapproved of the teaching, or the methods of discipline, or, if you had strong convictions about integration, that was all white. What happens is that sometimes a sense of guilt or anxiety about religious questions leads people to override their own instincts. While it's very appropriate to question and think about these things, which is the whole reason I did the book, people have to resolve it in terms of their own best judgment and their own best instincts, not thinking, "This is what I ought to do, because other people are doing it, or this is what has been done." For a large number of people, this probably does require quite a bit of wrestling, but then in the end they have to make the choice that corresponds to their own beliefs.

My advice is limited to this: Examine your own conscience, and then plunge ahead.

FI: Did writing the book affect how you feel about the way you're raising your child, and how confident you are in the way you're going about it?

FAY: I don't think it made me feel more confident; it made me feel more persuaded that I haven't any choice. This is indeed how I do feel, and there was never any real possibility of doing it any other way.

In the book, I was very honest about my own feelings, including in the passage on literature, where I talk about trying to read the Bible with my daughter. In fact, I do think the Bible is worth studying, something I wish I did know better. I don't know more about it because of the way I was raised, and I do have strong feelings about it being part of what a literate person should know. But I did feel ambivalent about how much of the moral teaching I could take, and how much I felt capable of interpreting for her.

That was a worthy attempt that other people had made, and I suspect that I wouldn't have explored it quite as intentionally if I hadn't been working on this book. It was the only thing I reached for because I had worked on this, that I thought about more analytically than I would have just as a parent.

You have to raise your child by your own example. You have to do it by constant attention to the issues that religion concerns itself with. If you're not talking about these things at home, if you're not answering your children's questions about the world and the way it works, the mystery, the injustice, nothing else will do that job. There's no free ride.

53

6

THE FEMINIST ICONOCLAST
An Interview with CAMILLE PAGLIA
Conducted by Timothy J. Madigan

One does not really interview Camille Paglia—author of the best-selling works
Sexual Personae; Sex, Art, and American Culture; *and* Vamps and Tramps—
one gives her a forum to express her free-wheeling opinions in machine-gun
delivery style on whatever issues she wants to address. What follows is a prime
example of what might be called her "in-your-face feminism."

FREE INQUIRY: You're one of the few public intellectuals whose work is discussed both on college campuses and in working-class bars. Why do you think you've touched such a nerve?

CAMILLE PAGLIA: It's pretty amazing. Don't forget by the time I burst on the scene five years ago, I was in my forties, and I'd gotten absolutely no attention whatsoever. I couldn't get published. Not only was *Sexual Personae* rejected by seven major publishing houses, but parts of it had been rejected for years by magazines.

But by the beginning of the 1990s, the culture seemed to change, and suddenly people were listening to me. There was a big shift. I represent the best of the 1960s, which was all about freethought and free speech. I hate dogma in any form. I hate it in the Roman Catholic church, which is why I left it twenty-five years ago. I hate it in gay activism and feminism now. Dogma has also taken over the humanities departments in elite schools—poststructuralism and so forth. I think people are sick of the ideological and clichéd ways in which cultural issues were approached in the 1980s. So I came like a breath of fresh air.

People who are interested in ideas welcomed me, and people who cling to a fixed belief system find me threatening. There's nothing more dangerous to a liberal democracy than fixed dogma. I don't like coteries. I have struggled

54

to maintain my outside position, which is very rare in America.

FI: In *Vamps and Tramps,* you state that "the silencing of authentic debate among feminists helps the rise of the far right."

PAGLIA: That's right, and the fruits of this are now being seen. I've warned about this for years—the suppression of debate by the liberal wing has moved the entire nation to the right. People who were surprised by the Republican sweep have simply not been listening to me. It happened not because of any right-wing conspiracy; it happened because of a spiritual vacuum on the left. The left became too removed from the people. Leftism began 150 years ago supposedly to speak for the silent majority, for the people. True sixties radicalism really was populist. I'm a Clinton supporter and I'll vote for him again (God help me), but he has surrounded himself with these white, upper middle class elite professionals who speak about "the people" from a very great distance and, in a very paternalistic, condescending way, as "victims." It is insulting—I'm remembering my background in an immigrant family when I say this—they are totally removed from the people they pretend to speak for. These false progressives are merely voices of reaction, clinging to outmoded, broken-down liberal ideas. After all, a lot of sixties radicalism was critical of the liberal establishment, like Leonard Bernstein having the Black Panthers over for tea—radical chic. Liberals were the worst hypocrites in the 1960s. I despise "limousine liberalism."

FI: You also say, "To rescue feminism, we must give religion its due, but require it to stay in its place."

PAGLIA: That has to be done to rescue all progressive politics. One of the major crises that the heirs to the left have received is the neglect of spiritual values. I'm an atheist, but we people of the sixties were very spiritual in our own ways. That is, we abandoned organized religions, but we sought out Hinduism and Buddhism. We were very interested in cross-cultural spiritual experiences. A passage to India, as it were.

Now what's happened as part of the collapse of the progressive left is a descent into social constructivism, which says that everything that we are is made by society. There's no feeling for nature anymore. The feminism that's being taught now is a very shrunken view of life. We are defined as nothing but social beings, the product of environmental pressures. There's a whole wing of feminism that insists there's no difference between male and female—we're exactly the same, and we become different because society shapes us in one direction or another. Gloria Steinem believes that, for example. There's another wing of feminism—the only one that does think of nature—and it sentimentalizes nature. It sees it as a wonderful goddess figure, and she's all good. I criticize that as being Rousseauist; and it's not true. The great fertility religions of the world have seen nature as having dual parts. Nature is a cycle of birth and death. It's positive and negative. Creative and destructive. There's a profound kind of collapse and contraction.

The Enlightenment turned away from organized religion, but put reason and science in its place. Romanticism rebelled against organized religion, but put nature and art in its place. What has modernism done? It has turned against organized religion, and given nothing in its place. The effects of this are being felt by the young today. Generation X. It's no coincidence that Kurt Cobain killed himself. What we have bequeathed is chaos to the young. The far right accurately observed the hollowness at the heart of our culture; but I disagree with the cure that the far right offers. What I'm saying to the left is, "Wake up! The far right sees something you are in denial about."

Everything is blighted for the young. They have reduced aspirations. They are in a dead end. Because of this total neglect of spiritual values we have the tremendous appeal of the right. There's two thousand years of developed thought behind Christianity. There's three thousand years behind Judaism. So, better Jehovah than Foucault. Jehovah at least brings along this incredible work, the Bible. What a great collection of poetry, magnificent, filled with things of spiritual use, whether you believe in God or not. The grandeur and intellectual development of Catholic theology is staggering. Foucault is a fraud; and that's the diet our best kids in the elite schools are being fed. It is appalling. The man knew nothing.

We have destroyed the young's natural instincts. We told them you cannot look at art without thinking of a prefab social agenda—racism, sexism, homophobia. We have destroyed the natural, pleasurable response to art. We've turned them into dried-up cynics. True creativity means being willing to make a fool of yourself, letting it all go.

The left is to be blamed for the appeal of the right. The right offers stable, traditional religious values. And when people marry and have children, they are concerned about what kind of values to give them. That's why so many people are turning back to the old religions. Religion has tremendous cultural power.

What I have offered in my work is a compromise solution. There should be shared educational experiences in all nations. The history of any culture is its religion. I'm looking for a scholarly view of religion. Everyone in the world should know Hinduism, Buddhism, Islam, Judeo-Christianity, African tribal religions, and so forth. What we would do in effect is say, "Here are all the possible ways of spiritually apprehending the universe."

Trying to produce an education that's completely clear of religion is stupid. It would be so easy for the left to say, "A moment of meditation in the schools is fine." What is the big deal? People who are religious can think religious thoughts. Let people just gather their thoughts.

I'm in the posture of attacking the left and saying to them "You have spawned Newt Gingrich." Rush Limbaugh is necessary. He's one of the few freethinkers in the whole culture. The people at Harvard, Princeton, Duke, and Stanford aren't freethinkers. They're just a bunch of lemmings compared to Rush Limbaugh, who's out there with his own independent point-of-view. He's a principled speaker and thinker, even though my politics are not his. The left can no longer claim to be the voice of the people.

FI: You also talk about a renewed interest in the pagan. Certainly organized religion had tried to eradicate pagan elements.

PAGLIA: The overall theme of my work is this: Judeo-Christianity never defeated paganism. Instead, paganism, after the fall of Rome, was driven underground, and it has erupted in Western culture at three key moments. The first was the Renaissance. Greco-Roman humanism came back—Botticelli did a painting of Venus rather than the Madonna. The second moment was Romanticism. And the most glamorous of my three eruptions is the twentieth century. I call it not Sartre's Age of Anxiety, but rather the Age of Hollywood. Modern popular culture is in fact an eruption of the buried pagan element in Western civilization—the very things the far right finds most unpalatable. Christianity has never been able to honestly deal with sex, because it belongs to the natural realm and Christianity imagines us as transcending our natural selves, becoming like God up in heaven who's sexless and bodiless. "Turn the other cheek" does not deal with the innateness of aggression. Many feminists believe one is taught to be violent by a violent society. Those things that people most deplore are precisely what the culture needs. It is the strange truncations, limitations, and repressions of Judeo-Christianity that have in fact produced the cult of the striving, heroic, turbulent individual artist, from Michelangelo to Baudelaire to Lord Byron down to Elvis Presley. This is part of the greatness of the West. It's based on neurosis and repression.

FI: The artists are somewhat like oysters producing pearls from the irritants of their upbringing.

PAGLIA: Judeo-Christian theology is fascinating—very complex, very intellectually stimulating. In some ways, it's an overdevelopment of one part of the brain, and the body suffers. We need a long view. But we're in a period of postmodernism, where people have this stupid idea that there are no great narratives anymore. Everything is discontinuous.

FI: Postmodernism seems to lead back to premodernism: questioning all the presumptions of modernism reawakens interest in ancient theologies.

PAGLIA: Postmodernism is a big fancy word for nothing. It is so passé.

Let's get past Beckett's *Waiting for Godot*. The view of the world that there's nothing but a nihilistic landscape is completely outmoded. That's not our world. I feel that African-American music has entered very deeply into our psyche. The negativity and alienation in the African-American experience is our native sensibility, and it's revolutionized the world in terms of music and dance. I'm trying to assassinate postmodernism. I'm at war with the people in our universities and academic journals and everywhere where people are still preaching this line. It's the worst thing in the world to say to someone, "The world is empty, the world is meaningless, no ideals are possible."

FI: Related to postmodernism is the claim that rational thinking is "phallocentric."

PAGLIA: Oh! That kind of talk is so embarrassing. It comes out of Jacques Lacan. Even the word *phallocentric* is such a stupid neologism. What kind of idiots do we have pretending that that is supposed to be a big philosophical term? All of Lacan's work is a big pile of manure as far as I'm concerned, completely useless. Thank God, when I entered college in 1964, I was exposed to great literature, great art, great thought, everything from Plato and Aristotle down to Hegel, Kant, Nietzsche, and Heidegger. People who use the word *phallocentric* are desperate academic careerists who want to sound important.

FI: Female writers who make these claims and refer to Lacan and Foucault don't seem to catch the irony that these are *male* thinkers telling them about "phallocentrism."

PAGLIA: Precisely. Most of the women in academe who pretend to be feminists are not. They do not know the history of feminism. They never studied history, anthropology, psychology, biology. And that is why, for all their attacks on the canon and tradition, they created an instant canon of their own, all the more false. I speak as a feminist. My feminism predates the feminism of Gloria Steinem. I go way back. Most of these women in my view have drifted from their own cultural or ethnic or religious identities and they cling to feminism as a new religion. That's why they are absolutely irrational when you try to argue with them. They have accepted passively certain received truths, and they have not thought them through. They cling together in bands, and never listen to anyone outside their group. They had the idea that if they ignored someone like me, I'd go away. It was perfect for me, because it allowed me to rampage unchecked. They're stupefied now. I have had three best-sellers in five years.

FI: Speaking of your tactics, you write that football is your only religion, and that feminists should learn strategies from it. Our editor Paul Kurtz published an article defending football in our Spring 1994 issue, and a lot of our

58

readers got very upset, accusing him of advocating violence.

PAGLIA: Ugggh. Baseball is a sport that all intellectuals pretend to like. It's very passive. I've never liked it, even though I played softball in school. But I love football. It's controlled violence. There are rules to circumscribe uncontrolled violence. You're penalized. I think that football is absolutely magnificent. I watched it with my father in Syracuse when I was young. The way the coaches and players strategize, plan, marshal the troops, anticipate, develop subterfuge—it's a wonderful combination of brain and brawn.

There's no doubt that I have modeled a lot of my tactics on football. When the academic feminists tried to stonewall me, I ran a misdirection play. My most notorious sentence is in the first chapter of *Sexual Personae*—"If civilization had been left in female hands, we would still be living in grass huts." I knew that this sentence would inflame these women, that they would not read my book, and I could stampede them to go in the wrong direction. They would assume that I was of the far right. They were absolutely convinced that they knew what my system was.

It worked brilliantly. I managed to evade early tackles. I had the field to myself for a long time. I often say, I modeled my hits—my one-line attack soundbites—on those great crisp hits in the middle of the field that you can hear all the way in the back row. I love that kind of style, where a free safety appears out of nowhere. I'm doing quick, sharp hits, very violent but also with great bravura. If I were to be asked what position I'd play it would be either free safety or tight end—those big guys who run right over people to the goal line. Football is a great model for keeping your vision, concentrating energy, planning, and keeping in condition.

FI: It would be nice if you could coach the Buffalo Bills. They might actually win a Super Bowl with your attitude.

You have a very Nietzschean element in your writing style—you, too, "philosophize with a hammer." You make many statements that are deliberately provocative. Here's one from *Vamps and Tramps:* "It's not male hatred of women, but male fear of woman that is the great universal."

PAGLIA: I think that that is my best contribution to feminism. When I came on the scene, all these wonderful archetypes from the whole of world history—the *femme fatale,* the medusa, the gorgon—were considered to be hallucinatory projections by women-hating men. And what I did was to recover the stereotypes and show that they contain some terrible truth about sexual relations. Take a film like *Basic Instinct,* which feminist and gay activists picketed. I loved *Basic Instinct.* I thought Sharon Stone gave one of the great performances in the history of film. She showed, in the interrogation scene where all the men are turned to jelly when she uncrosses her legs, that the sexual woman dominates man. She is in such command there. Men don't hate women. There are some men who hate their mothers—usually they end up being serial murderers.

Mostly men are fascinated by and fear women. Woman represents the origin of man—every boy comes out of a woman's body. It's beyond personality. It has to do with this huge force that is nature itself. Some feminism tries to cut us off from nature and says "We're just the same"—well, we're not just the same. Woman's reproductive capabilities are very mysterious. Science still can hardly come up with terms to analyze it. I regard man as peripheral, marginal, to this huge reality.

I got this idea from studying literature and art and realizing that so much of world mythology has certain shared themes. When you find something so widespread through so many periods, then you must say there is something to female sexuality that gives rise to these nightmare visions. I have a larger vision as a scholar, with a huge view of history—most of my opponents are pathetic. They know nothing. They might know modern periods, they might know the Renaissance, but they really do not have this broad overview.

Men do fear being sucked back into the womb again, shrunk down into infancy again. It's not clear how intimate men can be with women without masculinity being suffocated and terminated in women's greater power. This is a profound problem. A lot of behavior that looks like male domination, I began to realize, was part of the way that men keep themselves free. Masculinity is very very fragile. Men go directly from control by their mothers to control by their wives. They have one brief period when they're free, and that's when they run and rampage. We need to understand this. Warren Farrell, in his book *The Myth of Male Power,* says that "Female beauty is the world's most potent drug." That is so true, and feminism does not understand the allure that women have, that men are awed by women and then become defensive because they don't want to be castrated or become slaves to women. There's a real tension, back and forth through history.

I have a peculiar way of looking at things, through male eyes. It's probably because of my bisexual experience. Many of the things I'm saying are obvious, but feminism is so stuck behind its own blinders. One of the worst of these is to constantly see misogyny everywhere. I'm called a misogynist! Does that make any sense? Someone who's an open lesbian, who's written on Madonna and Diana and Elizabeth Taylor and Jackie Kennedy Onassis? I'm constantly writing evocatively of women.

By the way, I hope you will identify me as a feminist. Some people just carelessly call me an anti-feminist. Gloria Steinem just did that again recently in the *New York Times.* That is so stupid. I am a dissident feminist who is a critic of the feminist establishment. I'm someone who's trying to reform feminism, as much as my great heroine, St. Teresa of Avila, who wasn't trying to get rid of Catholicism, but was trying to reform it. Which she did. She was great trouble to the archbishop and the Catholic hierarchy, but she completely, single-handedly reformed the Spanish Carmelites. And that's what I feel I'm doing to feminism, and to academe.

7

FEMINISM, PRESENT AND FUTURE AN INTERVIEW WITH ELEANOR SMEAL

Eleanor ("Ellie") Smeal is one of the best-known figures in the modern move-ment for women's equality, gaining a reputation as a political strategist and grass-roots organizer. She served three terms as president of the National Or-ganization for Women, increasing its membership sixfold and transforming it into the nation's preeminent feminist organization. In 1987 she co-founded and became president of the Fund for the Feminist Majority and Feminist Ma-jority Foundation, which recruits feminists to run for public office and advo-cates gender balance laws for state and city boards and commissions.

This interview was conducted by Timothy J. Madigan.—EDS.

FREE INQUIRY: How do you respond to people who say this is a "post-feminist" era?

ELEANOR SMEAL: We never had a feminist era. If you look at a fem-inist era as one in which woman have achieved equality, we're obviously a long way away from it. The whole "post-feminist" rhetoric is more or less wishful thinking on the part of those who saw the sixties as a feminist era, and who are trying to write the women's movement out of the future. But the women's movement is very much alive and isn't about to go away.

FI: The word *feminism* itself is often tagged with the word *radical* in front of it.

SMEAL: I think this is wonderful, because those who do that know that feminism has a tremendously large following, really larger than any other subdivision like liberal or conservative, and certainly larger than most reli-gious denominations. They have to say it's those *radical* feminists they don't like, because they know doggone well that a huge portion of people believe in women's equality. Frankly, I think if you just ask the question, "Do you believe in equality?" the number of people who would answer "Yes" would go way up. Yet, that is the most difficult feminist issue, the fight for equality.

FI: One of the main tasks of *FI* is to critique claims of organized religion. I wonder if you can talk a bit about the ways in which organized religions currently are helping or hindering the feminist movement.

SMEAL: Some of the largest religious movements are fighting equality. The Catholic church is fighting the ordination of women priests and increasing women's leadership roles within the church. It is also, of course, leading the anti-abortion forces, which is one of the major women's rights issues. Many Protestant denominations have accepted women in the clergy, although not with open arms—many women find they can become ordained but cannot find a parish or congregation to lead. Orthodox Jews have still excluded us from the rabbinate, and fundamentalist Muslims are still fighting over whether women must wear the veil. Estimates run into the thousands as to how many women in Islamic countries have been killed for not wearing it.

FI: Is your organization in touch with feminists in Muslim countries?

SMEAL: Yes. We've been particularly interested in the veil issue, since it symbolizes the subjugation of women. In Algeria women have been killed even though moderates are still in control of the government. We've also been very active in the Taslima Nasrin case. We led a picket of the Bangladesh embassy and were told that that demonstration influenced the decision to release her.

FI: What about the recent Cairo conference on population and the attempts of religious groups to have their views prevail?

SMEAL: It's encouraging that the Vatican's attempt to forge an alliance with the Muslims failed. At the end the Vatican only had four countries voting with it. The document that came out of the conference is a testimony to the strength of the feminist movement worldwide, because it highlighted the need to increase women's rights if we're ever to stabilize the population of the world.

FI: What are your reflections on the recent [1994] congressional and state elections in the United States and how they will affect the drive for a feminist majority?

SMEAL: It is a disaster for a lot of women's issues, especially abortion. Forty-seven right-to-lifers are now estimated to be in the Senate, and in the House twenty-nine pro-choicers were defeated by pro-lifers. I estimate we lost about forty seats in the House and quite a few in the Senate. It's a very serious setback, especially considering the weakness of the current presidency.

On the other hand, I believe Congress is lagging behind the rest of the nation in supporting women's rights. Maybe this will create the momentum for more change.

I don't think we've seen the end of political change in this country. In fact, I think we're in a very turbulent time. We don't know yet how it's going to end. It's clear there is a big taxpayer's revolt, which the right wing is using to its advantage. What's fueling this whole conservative movement are the bad economic times.

Incidentally, feminists abroad tell us what's fueling the fundamentalist movement, for example in Muslim countries, is poverty. The biggest followers of fundamentalism are men who have lost jobs and who see no light at the end of the tunnel. They're being promised salvation when they can't cope in this world. They see feminism as part of the modern world that is cheating them. The modern woman has been made the scapegoat for the failed economy.

FI: In the United States, as more women enter the workforce, there becomes a sense of increased competition between men and women for jobs.

SMEAL: For the men who have failed to compete we've become the whipping person. A little bit of that can be seen in the Rush Limbaugh phenomenon, the laughing guy who bashes feminists and gays and anybody he thinks is not "normal." It's not necessarily low-income people who participate in these attacks. It's a way for threatened men to feel important.

FI: You've written about the different strategies used by Susan B. Anthony and Elizabeth Cady Stanton in combatting organized religion. How are they relevant today?

SMEAL: Stanton believed that churches—in that time primarily the Protestant ones—were determined to keep women in their place. And that unless you changed the notion of women's place in the Bible, you couldn't achieve equality. That's why she spent a great deal of her later life writing *The Woman's Bible,* reinterpreting the Bible to show that it was essentially rewritten to argue for woman's inequality. She felt that if you didn't fight woman's inequality in the church, you couldn't achieve equality in the greater society.

Susan B. Anthony thought it was dangerous to take on too many opponents—she thought temperance was important for woman's equality. She didn't see that that could be slowing up women's drive for the vote. Anti-temperance forces were behind the anti-woman's vote movement. They were afraid that if women got the vote they would outlaw liquor.

I think that same scenario is present today, where so many feminists and people in general are afraid to speak out on, for example, the Roman Catholic church's opposition to abortion or woman's equality. Not speaking out is costing us dearly. For example, there's a terrible silence in our progressive forces on pedophilia within the priesthood. Here's a church that says it has the moral answers for teenage girls, and yet has a gigantic moral scandal within its ranks.

FI: I suspect that such reports are nonetheless having a major impact on people within the church.

SMEAL: It's the biggest scandal since the Reformation, and the biggest challenge to date to the church's moral authority. Note the church's hypocrisy on homosexuality: a priest who died in a gay sauna in Ireland was given the last rites by two other priests who were there. But all that got was a little blurb in the Pittsburgh *Post Gazette.* Such incidents make a mockery of what the church is teaching, and church authorities need to address the issue much more vigorously. Newt Gingrich is now talking about orphanages and foster care run by churches. How can the church do that when it has a major pedophilia problem? What politician would point this out? I can guarantee you that if there were scandals like this among the feminist leadership, we'd be out of business.

FI: What are your views regarding reforming existing religions, with nonsexist language and female clergy? Are some of these institutions patriarchal by their nature?

SMEAL: One questions if such changes go to the very heart of theology. The language of mysticism has a lot of sexual allusions. The fight is much more vigorous than most would have thought.

I'd estimate that most of the women in theological training are feminists. Even most nuns are now predominantly feminist—I saw that report in a right-to-life publication! There is no question that the women religionists are a different breed than the men.

FI: Molleen Matsumura, our associate editor, has a sixteen-year-old daughter who, when she heard I was going to be interviewing you, wanted me to ask you this: "What do today's young feminists need to do to continue the movement's work of expanding women's identities and opportunities?"

SMEAL: The first thing to do is become involved in the movement. I hope they don't sit on the sidelines while history is being made—the women's movement will influence our culture more than any other movement.

If we could figure out how to organize more efficiently and effectively, we would reach equality. Our structures come from the turn of the century and need to change to work in modern times.

FI: Your answer applies to the humanist movement as well. It strikes us as very ironic that the forces advocating a backward-thinking message are using up-to-the-minute technology, while we're still pounding away on fifteen-year-old computers.

SMEAL: The problem here is money. Established interests are funding the fundamentalists. It's not that they're popular—they're funded. Let's remember, this election was not won on religious or social issues, but fear of crime, illegal immigrants, and not being prosperous. What gives them the appearance of popularity is their ability to communicate effectively to their minority audience. They have resources we don't. It is tragic that the money interests have bet on old, reactionary forces.

FI: We have to hope that this is the last gasp of the traditionalists.

SMEAL: I'm not that sanguine. I've seen far too much ability to slow down progress. We should have made far more gains than we have by now. We are still debating issues, like abortion rights, that should have been settled years ago.

If anything, it's because of the power of television and mass communication that it might be even easier to manipulate mass hysteria and emotions negatively. This is not a time for us to think, "Well, they'll be defeated, it's only a matter of time." It could be more than forty years from now, you know. That's why we'd better organize and work even harder than ever!

8

WORLD CITIZEN:
AN INTERVIEW WITH
SIR PETER USTINOV

Conducted by Warren Allen Smith

*U*pon *first meeting Sir Peter Ustinov, the Goodwill Ambassador-at-Large for UNICEF and president of the World Federalist Movement, one hears the voice of* Peter and the Wolf. *One feels the presence of Beethoven (from his stage performance in Beethoven's Tenth); of Carabosse (from the play,* The Love of Four Colonels*); of the General (from the film and play,* Romanoff and Juliet*); and of Nero (from his film role in* Quo Vadis*).*

Surprisingly, Ustinov, who amusingly responds "Your Excellency" when addressed as "Sir Peter," comes across as friendly, witty, ready to imitate the facial expressions of François Mitterrand, eloquent when discussing the world's children, and sincere when lamenting intolerance, bigotry, flag-waving, self-importance, idleness, and superstition. He is not intimidating, yet this is the man who has worked with Jack Paar, Steve Allen, Pavarotti, Herbert von Karajan, André Kostelanetz, David Niven, Yvonne de Carlo, Maggie Smith, Helen Hayes, Bette Davis, Nick Nolte, and John Gielgud. And the man who, in 1990, was knighted by Queen Elizabeth II.

Ustinov was in New York City in April to promote his new book, Ustinov Still At Large *(Prometheus Books, 1995), on national television and at book-stores. The London-born Ustinov agreed to an interview while his Parisian-born wife, Hélène du Lau d'Allemans, served champagne to their interviewer.*

First off, Ustinov had kind words for Paul Kurtz, editor of Free Inquiry, *and for Prometheus Books. Although he has never been "a joiner," he is a member of the Council for Secular Humanism's Academy of Humanism and an honorary associate of Britain's Rationalist Press Association.*

FREE INQUIRY: Your telecast "Inside the Vatican" got wide coverage here.

USTINOV: Yes. It was not uncritical, but was tactful.

FI: Do I understand that McGreevy Productions is working on a similar telecast?

USTINOV: We've just now done a history of the Greek gods, "Paths of Gods." It will show it's quite wrong to consider the Greek gods as being dead. One thing that ancient history proves is that virtue predates religion by a long way and that Socrates was a godly man and he didn't need a god to be that. The ancient gods were free from inhibition and free from guilt and free from all feeling of Original Sin, which came in with monotheism.

In a certain sense the ancients are much more up-to-date than the theistic churches, simply because they have affected and still affect psychiatry and psychoanalysis, which are very modern studies. Oedipus may have left us long ago, but he has left behind his complex. Achilles has left his heel. Aphrodite has left aphrodesiacs. Lethe has left weapons, the weapons of oblivion. And there is the Platonic relationship.

Moreover, the Greeks have much more to teach us than official religions, if we bother to study them. Witch-burnings and the Inquisition contrast with the Greeks' much more frivolous and pleasant approach, one which goes much further into the darkness of the human spirit. They delighted in life. Their dramas were followed then much as people today follow soap operas. When the Romans tolerated religion, they didn't, as in the fictions that are put out now, authorize Christian religion and become Christians themselves. In a much longer process, they decided to authorize *all* the religions, along with them the Christian religion. And it so happened that the Christian religion outlasted the others for a variety of reasons. But at least some of the Christian churches are relics of other temples.

FI: You observed a Mithraic temple that was buried underneath two layers of Christian churches?

USTINOV: Yes. Mithras was a deity akin to Apollo. Mithraism is quite interesting because it has the equivalents of the Crucifixion, Ascension, and Last Supper and all the stuff of Christianity, but just not the themes that go into Cecil B. DeMille's magic box. It's very extraordinary that all these myths seem to have a common base—even paganism, which has been borrowed from freely by the church, along with all the mess about the Dead Sea Scrolls.

FI: Your father was a liberal Lutheran and a journalist. Would he have been closer to Greek or Judeo-Christian thinking?

USTINOV: Oh, the Greeks! He was absolutely unpracticing in his belief.

68

In point of fact, it was his father who was so religious. His mother, and I remember her vividly because she was half Ethiopian, held religion very close, and for her the Crucifixion happened yesterday. I sat on her knee in my pajamas and had to listen to the history of the Crucifixion as though it had been brought in from Pittsburgh, and she used to cry copiously and my pajama tops were wet from her tears.

[He added that he fancies he got rheumatism at a young age because of that humidity, laughing that of course this is just his imagination. Ustinov, because of arthritis, now uses a regal-looking cane.]

FI: Before being knighted, you were a Commander of the British Empire. Another CBE, Arthur C. Clarke, holds that "it may be that our role on this planet is not to worship God . . . but to create him."

USTINOV: Well, I agree that it is inherent in human nature. And I have always said that I have much more faith in an agnostic or an atheist who helps an old lady across the road than the man who is racing to church and pretends not to see her. [He laughs.]

FI: Your new book, *Ustinov Still at Large,* is a compilation of articles you have written for *The European.*

USTINOV: The paper was owned by Robert Maxwell. He generously offered me six weeks of holiday each year but for four years I have never taken that vacation. In his obituary, I wrote: "There's absolutely no law against a crook having a good idea."

FI: Do you use a computer?

USTINOV: No, I still use a pencil and write in longhand. I phone the copy in from such remote spots as Central Siberia, Northern Thailand—and New York City. [Laughter.] My first columns were published as *Ustinov at Large.* The present volume is *Ustinov Still at Large.* Eventually, there'll be an *Ustinov Still at Large Again.*

FI: Have you ever put a label on your personal philosophy?

USTINOV: No, deliberately not. Because I have never belonged to anything. But I believe in my book about God and the Devil, *The Old Man and Mr. Smith,* there comes a moment when the Devil reflects near the end that it's really terrible to think about how many people have been tortured and killed because of their beliefs. Relatively few were killed for what they did, probably because those who did bad things were in a position to do them, like Hitler and Mussolini. Then God says something to the effect that, "Well, really, to My mind prayer is the only thing that's important. And when a man is praying you don't know from the outside what he is praying to. That's what makes people so jealous to know what they believe. But in point of fact it doesn't really matter whether it's Me or a volcano or a tree. The fact is that

that puts man into a relationship with the size of the universe, which is quite salutary because he doesn't believe—otherwise, he could go mad. And, really, once everything is Me, what's the difference between all these things? What's the difference between Me and the god with the clay feet? I'm everything according to the conventional belief, and, if that is so, then there is no heresy possible."

My point is that I have no proof of anything; therefore, I believe in what I see and what I feel. But of course I'm ready to be surprised at any moment. The world [laughs] should not be in that position.

FI: FREE INQUIRY is well-named then? We freely search for truths, not Truth, even if this involves changing our viewpoint.

USTINOV: Oh, I think that it's an honorable thing to change your mind occasionally. I don't think it's a sign of weakness or lack of integrity. I believe men are united by their doubts and separated by their convictions. Therefore, it's a very good thing to have doubts. Doubts are the greatest spur to activity that I know of.

FI: *Skeptical Inquirer,* the journal that investigates claims of the paranormal, contains many articles about such doubts. For example, there are stories concerning crying statues, UFOs, Big Foot marks in the snow, etc.

USTINOV: Oh, those Big Foot marks I know about. They're Yeltsin's, trying to find the bathroom at night. [Laughter.]

FI: In the 1930s, we humanists were alarmed about the growth in the world's population. Then there were 2 billion humans. In 1970 there were 3.7 billion. Now there are almost 6 billion.

USTINOV: Yes, when you see conditions in India, for instance, you simply can't believe as the pope does. If the critics bothered to travel in those parts of the world they'd have no two opinions about this. Those who attack the Draconian methods employed by the Chinese to limit their births have to admit that, up to a point, the measures paid off. They may seem like an imposition on personal liberties, but with a country of that size of population, which nobody else has, they have to do something. I think that a sense of responsibility should not be interpreted as a curb on human liberty. Sometimes it is absolutely essential to say this can't go on any further. In my recent newspaper columns, I express my depression that there is such an outcry about anti-abortion methods and the idea of abortion as being a betrayal of life. I'm depressed that once children are born they're so often neglected. And what is life then, something that is lived in third gear or only in first gear? Our responsibility should be with children, not merely with embryos.

FI: As UNICEF's Goodwill Ambassador you visit children all over the world?

USTINOV: Yes, and children are the one strata of life who have absolutely no prejudice. None of us, and this is a message of hope, are born with prejudice. You often see children playing with someone who is hideously deformed by some caprice of nature, and the only people appalled are the adults who are wondering whether the children should be allowed to play together.

Unfortunately, prejudice comes from education and family life and all the things that are praised by religious orthodoxy. Every good bottle of wine has to have some residue. Similarly, life comes with prejudice, and there's little one can do. I am still unlearning what I learned in my first school, for example. Why do I think that? I ask myself, and then trace it back to some idiotic history book or patriotic idea.

FI: Who in history would you have liked to spend an hour with? Jacqueline Onassis responded to such a question by answering Sergei Diaghilev. On your mother's side, don't you have a connection with that Russian ballet impressario and art critic?

USTINOV: Yes, my Great-Uncle Alexander Benois was one of Diaghilev's artistic mentors. When I first went on stage, he wrote me a charming letter saying that for more than two centuries the family had been prowling around theaters, building and designing them, composing and conducting in them, and now at last one had had the nerve to get up on the stage itself.

FI: And who would you have spent an hour with?

USTINOV: [*Hesitates.*] Well, Dostoevsky fascinates me because even in Russia's turmoil today you find the same cast and characters. Then there's Bolivar. And Beethoven—I wrote a play about him and portrayed him in German in Berlin. Also Gogol. I am fond of the Russians—my plays have been better performed there than anywhere else and always without benefit of my advice, which is a little irritating.

The hour went by all too quickly. Sir Peter needed to write his weekly newspaper column and prepare for his one-man show in Toronto and ceremonies at which he was to receive the Norman Cousins award from the World Federalists and a Rudolph Valentino award. Ah, the joys of deadlines, spotlights, ceremonies! Had life always been so happy? No, he confided; he once had had a nightmare. Robed men had come into his bedroom while he was sleeping. They announced that he had been elected, and he looked through a window and saw smoke rising from a chimney. He was asked what name he would pick now that he had been chosen. Realizing that there was no escape, he thought for a moment, then declared with conviction, "Pope Not Guilty!"

Few of us have had the good luck to spend an hour with a real live knight. If you have a chance to catch Sir Peter's one-man show or read his newspaper column or books, by all means do so. You'll find no knight on a white horse. He is, however, a connoisseur of automobiles. Someday you might glimpse him behind the wheel of his white 1927 Mercedes Benz.

9

THE MORAL CASE FOR ABORTION
Henry Morgentaler

Henry Morgentaler was born on March 19, 1923, in Lodz, Poland. From 1940–1945 he was interned in the Lodz Ghetto and in the Auschwitz and Dauchau concentration camps. He received his medical education in Germany, Belgium, and Montreal, Canada. In 1968, moved by the tragedies of women suffering injury and death in unsafe, illegal abortions, Morgentaler opened Canada's first abortion clinic, in Montreal. In 1973, he was tried on a charge of illegal abortion and acquitted by a jury. The jury acquittal was reversed by the Court of Appeal of Quebec. In 1975, this most unusual conviction was upheld by the Supreme Court of Canada. Morgentaler served ten months of an eighteen-month sentence when Canada's House of Commons passed the "Morgentaler Amendment," making it unconstitutional for the legislature to overturn a jury acquittal. In all, Morgentaler was tried four times on charges of illegal abortion. In 1988, the last attempted prosecution ended when the Supreme Court of Canada declared Canada's abortion law unconstitutional. Canada has since remained without any federal law governing abortion. Morgentaler has opened clinics across Canada, often in the face of strong provincial opposition. In 1992 his Toronto clinic was firebombed. No perpetrator was ever captured. Early in 1996, Morgentaler made headlines across Canada and internationally when he issued an open letter to Pope John Paul II, imploring the pontiff to reconsider traditional Catholic doctrines about abortion, birth control, and women's roles in society. He is the author of Abortion and Contraception *(1982). He is the founding president of the Humanist Association of Canada and has received awards from Planned Parenthood, the National Abortion Rights Action League (NARAL), the National Abortion Federation, the Council for Secular Humanism, and the International Humanist and Ethical Union.*

This is a very appropriate time for me to write on "The Moral Case for Abortion." Many people in the pro-choice community believe that the battle for reproductive freedom has been won, that abortion is now available, that women have gained control over their reproductive capacities and have been liberated from the repressive rulings of patriarchal governments. This is not completely true.

There are still many countries in the world where women are subjected to the dogmatic religious edicts of theocracies. There are still women willing to endanger their health, future fertility, and even their lives in order to terminate an unwanted pregnancy. The religious right and the anti-abortion movement is gaining ground on this continent and abroad. Even here, in the United States, where everyone hoped that *Roe* v. *Wade* would forever ensure a woman's right to choice, the violent factions of the anti-abortion movement are waging war on doctors, staff, and abortion clinics; and political lobby groups and presidential candidates violently opposed to choice are within reach of the Oval Office. There are even members of the pro-choice community who are questioning the morality of reproductive freedom. These people believe that abortion must be available, but that it is inherently bad—a necessary evil. This attitude is dangerous and destructive and undermines the enormous gains due to the availability of good abortion services. In fact, the decision to have an abortion is clearly an extremely moral choice; it is a choice that liberates, empowers, and benefits women and society. In this article, I will examine all these issues from a humanist perspective, and reaffirm the morality of reproductive choice.

The issue of the morality of abortion provides the best illustration of the profound difference between humanist ethics and traditional religious attitudes. The former are based on concern for individual and collective well-being and are able to incorporate all available modern data and knowledge; whereas the latter are bound by dogma and tradition to sexist, irrational prohibitions against abortion and women's rights and are completely and callously indifferent to the enormous, avoidable suffering such attitudes are inflicting on individuals and on the community.

Most of the debate raging about abortion around the world has centered around the question of morality. Is it ever moral or responsible for a woman to request and receive an abortion, or is abortion always immoral, sinful, and criminal?

When you listen to the rhetoric of the anti-abortion faction, or read imprecise terms about the unborn, you get the impression that every abortion kills a child; consequently it cannot be condoned under any circumstances, with the sole exception of when the life of the pregnant woman is endangered by the pregnancy, a condition that is now extremely rare. This position—that abortion is always wrong and that there is a human being in the womb from the moment of conception—is a religious idea mostly propagated by the doctrine of the Roman Catholic church and espoused by many fundamentalist Protestant groups, though not by the majority of Catholics and Protestants.

Let us briefly examine this idea. At the moment of conception the sperm and the ovum unite, creating one cell. To proclaim that this one cell is already a full human being and should be treated as such is so patently absurd that it is almost difficult to refute. It is as if someone claimed that one brick is already a house and should be treated with the same respect a full house deserves. Even if you have a hundred bricks, or two hundred bricks, it is not yet a house. For it to be a house it needs walls, plumbing, electricity, and a functional organization. The same is true for a developing embryo. In order for it to be a human being it needs an internal organization, organs, and especially a human brain to be considered fully human. This entity is the result of sexual intercourse, where procreation is often not the goal, and whether it is called a zygote, blastocyst, embryo, or fetus, it does not have all the attributes of a human being and thus cannot properly be considered one.

If abortion is always viewed as "intentional murder," why isn't miscarriage viewed in similar terms? After all, almost half of all embryos are spontaneously shed in what is called "miscarriage" or "spontaneous abortion." If spontaneous abortions are an "act of God," to use the common religious expression, is it not strange that God has so little concern for fetal life that He allows so much of it to go to waste without intervening? Is it not possible to then conclude that God does not mind or object to spontaneous abortions? Why is it that the Catholic church has no ritual to mark the abortion of so much fetal life when it occurs spontaneously, yet becomes so vociferous and condemnatory when it is a conscious decision by a woman or couple?

I believe that an early embryo may be called a *potential* human being. But remember that every woman has the potential to create twenty-five human beings in her lifetime. The idea that any woman who becomes pregnant as a result of non-procreative sexual intercourse *must* continue with her pregnancy does not take into consideration the fact that there is a tremendous discrepancy between the enormous potential of human fertility and the real-life ability of women and couples to provide all that is necessary to bring up children properly. The morality of any act cannot be divorced from the foreseeable consequences of that act. Should a girl of twelve or a woman of forty-five, or any woman for that matter, be forced to continue a pregnancy or be saddled with bringing up a child for eighteen years without any regard for the consequences, without any regard for the expressed will or desire of that woman, or of the couple?

Haven't we learned anything by observing events in countries where abortion is illegal, where women are forced to abort fetuses themselves or at the hands of quacks, where many die and more are injured for life or lose their fertility? What about the children often abandoned to institutions where they have no father or mother, where they suffer so much emotional deprivation and trauma that many become psychotic, neurotic, or so full of hate and violence that they become juvenile delinquents and criminals who kill, rape, and maim? When a person is treated badly in his or her childhood, that inner violence manifests itself when he or she is grown up.

The pro-choice philosophy maintains that the availability of good medical abortions protects the health and fertility of women and allows children to be born into homes where they can receive love, care, affection, and respect for their unique individuality, so that these children grow up to be joyful, loving, caring, responsible members of the community, able to enter into meaningful relationships with others.

Thus, reproductive freedom—access to legal abortions, to contraception, and, by extension, to sexual education—protects women and couples and is probably the most important aspect of preventive medicine and psychiatry, as well as the most promising preventative of crime and mental illness in our society.

Wherever abortion legislation has been liberalized, particularly in countries where abortion is available upon request, the effects on public health and on the well-being of the community have been very positive. The drastic reduction of illegal, incompetent abortions with their disastrous consequences has almost eliminated one of the major hazards to the lives and health of fertile women. There has been a steady decline in the complications and mortality associated with medical abortions, a decline in mortality due to childbirth, a drop in newborn and infant mortality, an overall decline in premature births, and a drop in the number of births of unwanted children. It is of utmost interest to examine the consequences and effects of the liberalization of the abortion laws.

Where abortion has become legalized and available and where there is sufficient medical manpower to provide quality medical services in this area, the consequences have all been beneficial not only to individuals but also to society in general. It countries where there is a high level of education and where abortions by qualified medical doctors are available without delay, self-induced or illegal abortions by incompetent people who do not have medical knowledge eventually disappear, with tremendous benefit to the health of women. Also, the mortality connected to medical legal abortions decreases to an amazing degree. In Czechoslovakia in 1978, for instance, the mortality rate was two per 100,000 cases; in the United States it was one death per 200,000 abortions, which is extremely low and compares favorably with the mortality rate for most surgical procedures.

Another medical benefit is that the mortality of women in childbirth also decreases in countries where abortion is legal and the medical manpower exists to provide quality services. This is because the high-risk patients like adolescents, older women, and women with diseases often choose not to continue a high risk pregnancy; consequently, the women who go through childbirth are healthier and better able to withstand the stresses of childbirth; thus, the infant mortality and neonatal mortality has decreased consistently in all countries where abortion has become available.

But probably the biggest benefit of legalized abortion and the one with the greatest impact is that the number of unwanted children is decreasing. Children who are abused, brutalized, or neglected are more likely to become neurotic, psychotic, or criminal elements of society. They become individuals who do not care about themselves or others, who are prone to violence, who are filled with hatred for society and for other people; if the number of such individuals decreases, the welfare of society increases proportionately.

One of the most surprising and beneficial changes going on in both the United States and Canada has been the tremendous decrease in crime, especially violent crime such as murder, rape and aggravated assault. This trend over the last four years has been proven by impressive statistics collected by the Federal Bureau of Investigation and the police forces of the United States and Canada. The decrease in violent crime is about 8% every year over the last four years. That is quite an impressive trend. Statistics from the province of Quebec, just released April 4, 1996, show a decrease in criminal offenses of 15% every year over the last three years and a decrease of 8% for violent crime. There has been a 30% decrease in crime in New York State, *e.g.* and many similar statistics in other areas are surprising and extraordinary in view of the prevailing economic uncertainties and disruptions of modern life. What is the explanation?

Some demographers explain this by the fact that there are fewer young men around, and it is mostly young men who commit crimes. No doubt this is true, but what is even more important is that among these young men likely to commit offenses there are fewer who carry an inner rage and vengeance in their hearts from having been abused or cruelly treated as children. Why is that? Because many women who a generation ago were obliged to carry any pregnancy to term now have had the opportunity to choose medical abortion when they were not ready to assume the burden and obligations of motherhood.

Crimes of violence are very often perpetrated by persons who unconsciously want revenge for the wrongs they suffered as children. This need to satisfy an inner urge for vengeance results in violence against children, women, members of minority groups, or anyone who becomes a target of hate by the perpetrator. Children who have been deprived of love and good care, who have been neglected or abused, suffer tremendous emotional harm that may cause mental illness, difficulty in living, and an inner rage that eventually erupts in violence when they become adolescents and adults.

Most of the serial killers were neglected and abused children, deprived of love. Paul Bernardo and Clifford Olson would fit in that category. Both Hitler and Stalin were cruelly beaten by their fathers and carried so much hate in their hearts that when they attained power they caused millions of people to die without remorse. It is accepted wisdom that prevention is better than a cure. To prevent the birth of unwanted children by family planning, birth control, and abortion is preventive medicine, preventive psychiatry, and prevention of violent crime.

I predicted a decline in crime and mental illness twenty-five years ago when I started my campaign to make abortion in Canada iegal and safe. It took a long time for this prediction to come true. I expect that conditions will get better as more and more children are born into families that want and deserve them with joy and anticipation.

It is safe to assume that there has been a similar decrease in mental and emotional illness due to the fact that fewer unwanted children are being born. Consequently fewer children suffer the emotional deprivation or abuse that is often associated with being unwanted and undesired. It would be interesting to see appropriate studies to that effect, and I postulate that they would show a dramatic decrease in the overall incidence of mental illness.

Medical abortions on request and good quality care in this area are a tremendous advance not only toward individual health and the dignity of women, but also toward a more loving, caring, and more responsible society, a society where cooperation rather than violence will prevail. Indeed, it may be our only hope to survive as a human species and to preserve intelligent life on this planet in view of the enormous destructive power that mankind has accumulated.

The right to legal abortion is a relatively new achievement, only about twenty-five years old in most countries. It is part of the growing movement of women toward emancipation, toward achieving equal status with men, toward being recognized as full, responsible, equal members of society. We are living in an era where women, especially in the Western world, are being recognized as equal, where the enormous human potential of womankind is finally being acknowledged and accepted as a valuable reservoir of talent. However, women cannot achieve their full potential unless they have freedom to control their bodies, to control their reproductive capacity. Unless they have access to safe abortions to correct the vagaries of biological accidents, they cannot pursue careers, they cannot be equal to men, they cannot avail themselves of the various opportunities theoretically open to all members of our species. The emancipation of women is not possible without reproductive freedom.

The full acceptance of women might have the enormous consequence of humanizing our species, possibly eliminating war and conflict, and adding a new dimension to the adventure of mankind. Civilization has had many periods of advance and regression, but overall it has seen an almost steady progression toward the recognition of minorities as being human and their acceptance into the overall community. It has happened with people of different nationalities and races. It has happened with prisoners of war, who could be treated mercilessly. It has happened quite recently, actually, with children, who were in many societies considered the property of parents and could be treated with brutality and senseless neglect. It is only a few generations ago that we recognized how important it is for society to treat children with respect, care, love, and affection, so that they become caring, loving, affectionate, responsible adults.

Finally, many countries now recognize the rights of women to belong fully to the human species, and have given them freedom from reproductive bondage and allowed them to control their fertility and their own bodies. This is a revolutionary advance of great potential significance to the human species. We are in the middle of this revolution, and it is not surprising that many elements of our society are recalcitrant and are obstructing this progress. They act out of blind obedience to dogma, tradition, and past conditions and are hankering for the times when women were oppressed and considered only useful for procreation, housework, and the care of children.

The real problems in the world—starvation, misery, poverty, and the potential for global violence and destruction—call for concerted action on the part of governments, institutions, and society at large to effectively control overpopulation. It is imperative to control human fertility and to only have children who can be well taken care of, receiving not only food, shelter, and education, but also the emotional sustenance that comes from a loving home and parents who can provide love, affection, and care.

In order to achieve this, women across the world have to be granted the rights and dignity they deserve as full members of the human community. This would naturally include the right to safe medical abortions on request in an atmosphere of acceptance of specifically female needs and in the spirit of the full equality of women and men in a more human and humane society.

Somebody has said that it is impossible to stop the success of an idea whose time has come. But good ideas come and go. Occasionally they are submerged for long periods of time due to ignorance, tradition, resistance to change, and the vested interests of those frightened by change. Occasionally, new and good ideas will gain slow and grudging acceptance. More often, they will be accepted only after a period of struggle and sacrifice by those who are convinced of the justice of their cause. The struggle for reproductive freedom, including the right to a safe, medical abortion, could be classified as one of those great ideas whose time has come.

Enormous progress has been made in many countries, including the United States and Canada. But in many other countries, legal abortion is still not available. With the beneficial effects of women's access to abortion and reproductive freedom so obvious to so many people, why is there still so much violent opposition to it? I believe it is due to the fact that people who are bound to traditional religious attitudes resent the newly acquired freedom of women and want to turn the clock back.

Taboos and practices regarding human reproduction and sexuality were written into religious teachings hundreds of years ago, which were then written into the laws of the country. Laws on abortion were introduced long before science enlightened us with the facts concerning embryological development. For instance, in the Catholic church it was thought that, at the moment of conception, a fully formed person, termed a *homunculus,* lived in the mother's womb, and had only to develop to a certain size to be expelled from it. That belief was held in the distant past, but the effect of the imagery still remains, resulting in the Catholic belief that abortion is the murder of a live human being.

Historically, and even up to this day, men hold the authority in all the major religions of the world. In most countries men are also heads of state and lawmakers. In science and medicine, men traditionally hold the reigns of authority and power, only recently allowing women entry into these fields. Is it any wonder then, that laws and attitudes regarding abortion took so long the change? But now these attitudes are changing, and women around the world are gradually acquiring more power and more control of their reproductive capacities. Unfortunately, organized religions, propelled by traditional dogma and fundamentalist rhetoric, are fueling the fires of the anti-choice movement with lying, inflammatory propaganda and violent rhetoric leading to riots and murder. The anti-choice supporters realize they have lost the battle, that public opinion has not been swayed by their diatribes and dogmatic opposition. Consequently, they are angry and increasingly engaging in terrorist tactics. Their recourse to violence, both in the United States and Canada, resulting in the murder and wounding of doctors performing abortions and the increasing violence directed at abortion providers, is a sign of moral bankruptcy, but unfortunately it places the lives of all physicians and medical staff who provide abortions in danger.

For those who believe that the so-called pro-life have occupied the high moral ground in the debate on abortion, I say, "Rubbish." They have never been on a high moral ground, they only pretend to occupy this elevated position by cloaking their oppressive beliefs under the lofty rhetoric of "the defense of innocent unborn life" or "the struggle against the death dealing abortion industry" and similar misleading and blatantly false propaganda. As well, the recourse by the anti-choice movement to violence and murder in order to impose their so-called morality on the whole of society certainly robs them of any credibility. In view of this, it is hard for me to understand the defeatist attitude of some people in the pro-choice community in the United States and their attempt to justify abortion as a necessary evil for which we should all apologize.

When a feminist with impressive credentials and many books to her credit such as Naomi Wolf talks of abortion as a "sin or frivolous," starts feeling guilty about it, and wants everyone who is engaged in providing abortions to repent for their sins, there is something definitely wrong. Were she alone I could believe it is a personal idiosyncrasy. However, there are others in the pro-choice community who attempt to justify themselves and their actions with an attitude that says, "Yes, we need abortions to help some women, but we deplore the fact that we have to do them, our hearts are not really in it, and it would be nice if we did not have to do it."

What is going on here? Have all these people forgotten that women used to die in our countries from self-induced or quack abortions, that unwanted children were given away to institutions where they suffered enormous trauma that took the joy of life away from them and made them into anxious, depressed individuals with a grudge against society? Have all these people forgotten that an unwanted pregnancy was the biggest health hazard to young fertile women and could result in loss of fertility, long-term illness, injury, and death?

Let us keep in mind the positive accomplishments of reproductive freedom that I mentioned earlier. An abortion need not be a traumatic event; it often is a liberating experience for the woman, who is able to make an important decision in her life, who exercises her right to choose what is best for her. That is the meaning of freedom, of empowerment.

A woman's choice to terminate a pregnancy is both empowering and liberating. It empowers her because her choice acknowledges that she understands her options, her current situation, and her future expectations, and she is able to make a fully informed decision about what would most benefit her and act on it. It liberates her because she can regain control of her reproductive system and chart her destiny without an unwanted child in tow. It liberates her to fully care for her existing family, her career, her emotional and mental well-being, and her goals.

It is our job as abortion providers to respect the choices of women and to provide abortion services with competence, compassion, and empathy. I wish to suggest that under such conditions women do not necessarily view their abortion as negative, but, on the contrary, and in spite of regrets at having to make such a choice, see it as a positive and enriching experience where their choices are respected and they are treated with the dignity they deserve in such a difficult situation.

Doctors and clinic workers have been in a stressful situation for many years, subject to threats, insults, and moral condemnation. Over the last four years the threats have escalated from verbal abuse to murder. Yet most of us have not given up. Most of us continue to provide excellent abortion services to women in spite of all the threats because we are committed to protection of women's health and to the liberation of women, to the empowerment of women and couples, and to a better society with freedom for all. I wish to salute all those health professionals who, in spite of intimidation and threats of death, are continuing every day to treat women with competence, empathy, and compassion.

I wish to conclude on a personal note. Over the years many people have asked me: "Why did you decide to expose yourself to so much stress and danger in a controversial cause, and why do you persist in doing so?" The answer, after a great deal of reflecting upon it, is the following:

I am a survivor of the Nazi Holocaust, that orgy of cruelty and inhumanity of man to man. As such, I have personally experienced suffering, oppression, and justice inflicted by men beholden to an inhuman, dogmatic, irrational ideology. To relieve suffering, to diminish oppression and injustice, is very important to me. Reproductive freedom and good access to medical abortion means that women can give life to wanted babies at a time when they can provide love, care, and nurturing. Well-loved children grow into adults who do not build concentration camps, do not rape, and do not murder. They are likely to enjoy life, to love and care for each other and the larger society.

By fighting for reproductive freedom, I am contributing to a more caring and loving society based on the ideals of peace, justice and freedom, and devoted to the full realization of human potential. Having known myself the depth of human depravity and cruelty, I wish to do whatever I can to replace hate with love, cruelty with kindness, and irrationality with reason.

This is why I so passionately dedicated to the cause I defend and why I will continue to promote it as long as I have a valid contribution to offer.

10

SACRED COW: THE DARK SIDE OF MOTHER TERESA
An Interview with Christopher Hitchens

Below, Matt Cherry, executive director of the Council for Secular Humanism, interviews Christopher Hitchens about his book The Missionary Position: Mother Teresa in Theory and Practice *(Verso, 1995) and his television program, which strongly criticized Mother Teresa. The interview recapitulates the most devastating critiques of Mother Teresa ever made. It also gives a very telling account, by a leading journalist, into the U.S. media's great reluctance to criticize religion and religious leaders.*

Christopher Hitchens is "Critic at Large" for Vanity Fair, *writes the Minority Report column for* The Nation, *and is a frequent guest on current affairs and commentary television programs. He has written numerous books on international current affairs, including* Blood, Class and Nostalgia: Anglo-American Ironies.

—EDS.

FREE INQUIRY: According to polls, Mother Teresa is the most respected woman in the world. Her name is a by-word for selfless dedication in the service of humanity. So why are you picking on this sainted old woman?

CHRISTOPHER HITCHENS: Partly because that impression is so widespread. But also because the sheer fact that this is considered unquestionable is a sign of what we are up against, namely the problem of credulity. One of the most salient examples of people's willingness to believe anything if it is garbed in the appearance of holiness is the uncritical acceptance of the idea of Mother Teresa as a saint by people who would normally be thinking—however lazily—in a secular or rational manner. In other words, in every sense it is an unexamined claim.

It's unexamined journalistically—no one really takes a look at what she does. And it is unexamined as to why it should be she who is spotlighted as opposed to many very selfless people who devote their lives to the relief of suffering in what we used to call the "Third World." Why is it never mentioned that her stated motive for the work is that of proselytization for religious fundamentalism, for the most extreme interpretation of Catholic doctrine? If you ask most people if they agree with the pope's views on population, for example, they say they think they are rather extreme. Well here's someone whose life's work is the propagation of the most extreme version of that.

That's the first motive. The second was a sort of journalistic curiosity as to why it was that no one had asked any serious questions about Mother Teresa's theory or practice. Regarding her practice, I couldn't help but notice that she had rallied to the side of the Duvalier family in Haiti, for instance, that she had taken money—over a million dollars—from Charles Keating, the Lincoln Savings and Loans swindler, even though it had been shown to her that the money was stolen; that she has been an ally of the most reactionary forces in India and in many other countries; that she has campaigned recently to prevent Ireland from ceasing to be the only country in Europe with a constitutional ban on divorce, that her interventions are always timed to assist the most conservative and obscurantist forces.

FI: Do you think this is because she is a shrewd political operator or that she is just naïve and used as a tool by others?

HITCHENS: I've often been asked that. And I couldn't say from real acquaintance with her which view is correct, because I've only met her once. But from observing her I don't think that she's naïve. I don't think she is particularly intelligent or that she has a complex mind, but I think she has a certain cunning.

Her instincts are very good: she seems to know when and where she might be needed and to turn up, still looking very simple. But it's a long way from Calcutta to Port au Prince airport in Haiti, and it's a long way from the airport to the presidential palace. And one can't just, in your humble way and dressed in a simple sari, turn up there. Quite a lot of things have to be arranged and thought about and allowed for in advance. You don't end up suddenly out of sheer simple naïveté giving a speech saying that the Duvalier family love the poor. All of that involves quite a high level of planning and calculation. But I think the genius of it is to make it look simple.

One of Mother Teresa's biographers—almost all the books written about her are by completely uncritical devotees—says, with a sense of absolute wonderment, that when Mother Teresa first met the pope in the Vatican, she arrived by bus dressed only in a sari that cost one rupee. Now that would be my definition of behaving ostentatiously. A normal person would put on at least her best scarf and take a taxi. To do it in the way that she did is the reverse of the simple path. It's obviously theatrical and calculated. And yet it is immediately written down as a sign of her utter holiness and devotion. Well, one doesn't have to be too cynical to see through that.

FI: You point out that, although she is very open about promoting Catholicism, Mother Teresa has this reputation of holiness amongst many non-Catholics and even secular people. And her reputation is based upon her charitable work for the sick and dying in Calcutta. What does she actually do there? What are her care facilities like?

HITCHENS: The care facilities are grotesquely simple: rudimentary, unscientific, miles behind any modern conception of what medical science is supposed to do. There have been a number of articles—I've collected some more since my book came out—about the failure and primitivism of her treatment of lepers and the dying, of her attitude towards medication and prophylaxis. Very rightly is it said that she tends to the dying, because if you were doing anything but dying she hasn't really got much to offer.

This is interesting because, first, she only proclaims to be providing people with a Catholic death, and, second, because of the enormous amounts of money mainly donated to, rather than raised by, her Order. We've been unable to audit this—no one has ever demanded an accounting of how much money has flowed in her direction. With that money she could have built at least one absolutely spanking new, modern teaching hospital in Calcutta without noticing the cost.

The facilities she runs are as primitive now as when she first became a celebrity. So that's obviously not where the money goes.

FI: How much money do you reckon she receives?

HITCHENS: Well, I have the testimony of a former very active member of her Order who worked for her for many years and ended up in the office Mother Teresa maintains in New York City. She was in charge of taking the money to the bank. She estimates that there must be $50 million in that bank account alone. She said that one of the things that began to raise doubts in her mind was that the Sisters always had to go around pretending that they were very poor and they couldn't use the money for anything in the neighborhood that required alleviation. Under the cloak of avowed poverty they were still soliciting donations, labor, food, and so on from local merchants. This she found as a matter of conscience to be offensive.

Now if that is the case for one place in New York, and since we know what huge sums she has been given by institutions like the Nobel Peace committee, other religious institutions, secular prize-giving organizations, and so on, we can speculate that if this money was being used for the relief of suffering we would be able to see the effect.

FI: So the $50 million is a very small portion of her wealth?

HITCHENS: I think it's a *very* small portion, and we should call for an audit of her organization. She carefully doesn't keep the money in India because the Indian government requires disclosure of foreign missionary organizations' funds.

I think the answer to questions about her wealth was given by her in an interview where she said she had opened convents and nunneries in 120 countries. The money has simply been used for the greater glory of her order and the building of dogmatic, religious institutions.

FI: So she is spending the money on her own order of nuns? And that order will be named after her?

HITCHENS: Both of those suggestions are speculation, but they are good speculation. I think the order will be named after her when she becomes a saint, which is also a certainty: she is on the fast track to canonization and would be even if we didn't have a pope who was manufacturing saints by the bushel. He has canonized and beatified more people than eight of his predecessors combined.

FI: Hence the title of your book: *The Missionary Position.*

HITCHENS: That has got some people worked up. Of the very, very few people who have reviewed this book in the United States, one or two have objected to that title on the grounds that it's "sophomoric." Well, I think that a triple *entendre* requires a bit of sophistication.

FI: And your television program in the United Kingdom was called "Hell's Angel."

HITCHENS: Yes, very much over my objection, because I thought that that name had not even a single *entendre* to it. I wanted to call it "Sacred Cow." The book is the television program expanded by about a third. The program was limited by what we could find of Mother Teresa's activities recorded on film. In fact, I was delighted by how much of her activity was available on film: for example, her praising the Albanian dictator Enver Hoxha. There is also film of her groveling to the Duvaliers: licking the feet of the rich instead of washing the feet of the poor. But "60 Minutes" demanded a price that was greater than the whole cost of the rest of the production. So we had to use stills.

FI: How did Mother Teresa become such a great symbol of charity and saintliness?

HITCHENS: Her break into stardom came when Malcolm Muggeridge—a very pious British political and social pundit—adopted her for his pet cause. In 1969, he made a very famous film about her life—and later a book—called *Something Beautiful for God*. Both the book and the film deserve the label hagiography.

Muggeridge was so credulous that he actually claimed that a miracle had occurred on camera while he was making the film. He claimed that a mysterious "kindly light" had appeared around Mother Teresa. This claim could easily be exploded by the testimony of the cameraman himself: he had some new film stock produced by Kodak for dark or difficult light conditions. The new stock was used for the interview with Mother Teresa. The light in the film looked rather odd, and the cameraman was just about to say so when Muggeridge broke in and said, "It's a miracle, it's divine light."

FI: Are we all victims of the Catholic public relations machine? Or has the West seized upon Mother Teresa as salve for its conscience?

HITCHENS: Well, you are giving me my answer in your question. For a long time the church was not quite sure what to do about her. For example, when there was the Second Vatican Council, in the 1960s, there was an equivalent meeting for the Catholics of the Indian subcontinent in Bombay. Mother Teresa turned up and said she was absolutely against any reconsideration of doctrine. She said we don't need any new thinking or reflection, what we need is more work and more faith. So she has been recognized as a difficult and dogmatic woman by the Catholics in India for a long time.

I think there were others in the church who suspected she was too ambitious, that she wouldn't accept discipline, that she wanted an order of her own. She was always petitioning to be able to go off and start her own show. Traditionally, the church has tended to suspect that kind of excessive zeal. I think it was an entirely secular breakthrough sponsored by Muggeridge, who wasn't then a Catholic.

So it wasn't the result of the propaganda of the Holy Office. But when the Catholic church realized it had a winner on its hands, it was quick to adopt her. She is a very great favorite of the faithful and a very good advertisement to attract non-believers or non-Catholics. And she's very useful for the current pope as a weapon against reformists and challengers within the church.

As to why those who would normally consider themselves rationalists or skeptics have fallen for the Mother Teresa myth, I think there is an element of post-colonial condescension involved, in that most people have a slightly bad conscience about "the wretched of the Earth" and they are glad to feel that there are those who will take action. Then also there is the general problem of credulity, of people being willing—once a reputation has been established—to judge people's actions by that reputation instead of the reputation by that action.

FI: Why do you think no other major media before you had exposed Mother Teresa?

HITCHENS: I'm really surprised by it. And also I'm surprised that no one in *our* community—that of humanists, rationalists, and atheists—had ever thought of doing it either.

There's a laziness in my profession, of tending to make the mistake I just identified of judging people by their reputation. In other words, if you call Saudi Arabia a "moderate Arab state" that's what it becomes for reportorial purposes. It doesn't matter what it does, it's a "moderate state." Similarly for Mother Teresa: she became a symbol for virtue, so even in cartoons, jokes, movies, and television shows, if you want a synonym for selflessness and holiness she is always mentioned.

It's inconvenient if someone robs you of a handy metaphor. If you finally printed the truth it would mean admitting that you missed it the first, second, and third time around. I've noticed a strong tendency in my profession for journalists not to like to admit that they ever missed anything or got anything wrong.

I think this is partly the reason, although in England my book got quite well reviewed because of the film, in the United States there seems to be the view that this book isn't worth reviewing. And it can't be for the usual reasons that the subject is too arcane and only of minority interest, or that there's not enough name recognition.

I believe there's also a version of multi-culturalism involved in this. That is to say, to be a Catholic in America is to be a member of two kinds of community: the communion of believers and the Catholic community, which is understood in a different sense, in other words, large numbers of Irish, Italian, Croatian, and other ethnic groups, who claim to be offended if any of the tenets of their religion are publicly questioned. Thus you are in a row with a community if you choose to question the religion. Under one interpretation of the rules of multi-culturalism that is not kosher: you can't do that because you can't offend people in their dearest identity. There are some secular people who are vulnerable to that very mistake.

I'll give you an interesting example, Walter Goodman, the *New York Times* television critic, saw my film and then wrote that he could not understand why it was not being shown on American television. He laid down a challenge to television to show this film. There was then a long silence until I got a call from Connie Chung's people in New York. They flew me up and said they would like to do a long item about the program, using excerpts from it, interviewing me and talking about the row that had resulted. They obviously wanted to put responsibility for the criticism of Mother Teresa onto me rather than adopt it themselves—they were already planning the damage control.

But they didn't make any program. And the reason they gave me was that they thought that if they did they would be accused of being Jewish and attacked in the same way as the distributors of *The Last Temptation of Christ* had been. And that this would stir up Catholic-Jewish hostility in New York. It was very honest of them to put it that way. They had already imagined what might be said and the form it might take and they had persuaded themselves that it wasn't worth it.

FI: So your film has never been shown in the United States?

HITCHENS: No, and it certainly never will be. You can make that prediction with absolute certainty; and then you can brood on what that might suggest.

FI: What was the response in Britain to your exposé of Mother Teresa? Did you get a lot of criticism for it?

HITCHENS: When the film was shown, it prompted the largest number of phone calls that the channel had ever logged. That was expected. It was also expected that there would be a certain amount of similarity in the calls. I've read the log, and many of the people rang to say exactly the same thing, often in the same words. I think there was an element of organization to it.

But what was more surprising was that it was also the largest number of calls in favor that the station had ever had. That's rare because it's usually the people who want to complain who lift the phone; people who liked the program don't ring up. That's a phenomenon well known in the trade, and it's a reason why people aren't actually all that impressed when the switchboard is jammed with protest calls. They know it won't be people calling in to praise and they know it's quite easy to organize.

A really remarkable number of people rung in to say it's high time there was a program like this. The logs scrupulously record the calls verbatim, and I noticed that the standard of English and of reasoning in the pro calls was just so much higher as to make one feel that perhaps all was not lost.

In addition to the initial viewer response, there was also a row in the press. But on the whole both sides of the case were put. Nonetheless, it was depressing to see how many people objected not to what was said but to its being said at all. Even among secular people there was an astonishment, as if I really had done something iconoclastic. People would say "Christopher Hitchens *alleges* that Mother Teresa keeps company with dictators" and so on, as though it hadn't been proven. But none of the critics have ever said, even the most hostile ones, that anything I say about her is untrue. No one has ever disproved any of that.

Probably the most intelligent review appeared in the *Tablet*, a English monthly Catholic paper. There was a long, serious and quite sympathetic review by someone who had obviously worked with the church in India and knew Mother Teresa. The reviewer said Mother Teresa's work and ideology do present some problems for the faith.

FI: But in America the idea that Mother Teresa is a sacred cow who must not be criticized won out and your book and your critique of Mother Teresa never got an airing?

HITCHENS: Yes, pretty much. Everything in American reviews depends on the *New York Times Book Review.* My book was only mentioned in the batch of short notices at the end. Considering that Mother Teresa had a book out at the same time, I thought this was very strange. Any book review editor with any red corpuscles at all would put both books together, look up a reviewer with an interest in religion and ask him or her to write an essay comparing and contrasting them. I have been a reviewer and worked in a newspaper office, and that is what I would have expected to happen. That it didn't is suggestive and rather depressing.

FI: The Mother Teresa myth requires the Indians to play the role of the hapless victims. What do the Indians think of Mother Teresa and of the image she gives of India?

HITCHENS: I've got an enormous pile of coverage from India, where my book was published. And the reviews seem to be overwhelmingly favorable. Of course it comes at a time when there is a big crisis in India about fundamentalism and secularism.

There are many Indians who object to the image of their society and its people that is projected. From Mother Teresa and from her fans you would receive the impression that in Calcutta there is nothing but torpor, squalor, and misery, and people barely have the energy to brush the flies from their eyes while extending a begging bowl. Really and truly that is a slander on a fantastically interesting, brave, highly evolved, and cultured city, which has universities, film schools, theaters, book shops, literary cafes, and very vibrant politics. There is indeed a terrible problem of poverty and overcrowding, but despite that there isn't all that much mendicancy. People do not tug at your sleeve and beg. They are proud of the fact that they don't.

The sources of Calcutta's woes and miseries are the very overpopulation that the church says is no problem, and the mass influx of refugees from neighboring regions that have been devastated by religious and sectarian warfare in the name of God. So those who are believers owe Calcutta big time, they should indeed be working to alleviate what they are responsible for. But the pretense that they are doing so is a big fraud.

FI: You mention in your book that Mother Teresa is used by the Religious

Right and fundamentalist Protestants who traditionally are very anti-Catholic as a symbol of religious holiness with which to beat secular humanists.

HITCHENS: Yes, she's a poster girl for the right-to-life wing in America. She was used as the example of Christian idealism and family values, of all things, by Ralph Reed—the front man of the Pat Robertson forces. That's a symptom of a wider problem that I call "reverse ecumenicism," an opportunist alliance between extreme Catholics and extreme Protestants who used to exclude and anathematize one another.

In private Pat Robertson has nothing but contempt for other Christian denominations, including many other extreme Protestant ones. But in public the Christian Coalition stresses that it is very, very keen to make an alliance with Catholics. There is a shallow, opportunist ecumenicism among religious extremists, and Mother Teresa is quite willingly and happily in its service. She knows exactly who she is working for and with. But I think she is happiest when doing things like going to Ireland and intervening in the Divorce Referendum, as she did recently.

By the way, there is an interesting angle to that which has not yet appeared in print. During the Divorce Referendum the Irish Catholic church threatened to deny the sacrament to women who wanted to be remarried. There were no exceptions to be allowed: it didn't matter if you had been married to an alcoholic who beat you and sexually assaulted your children, you were not going to get a second chance in this world or the next. And that is the position that Mother Teresa intervened in Ireland to support.

Now shift the scene: Mother Teresa is a sort of confessor to Princess Diana. They have met many times. You can see the mutual interest; I'm not sure which of them needs the other the most. But Mother Teresa was interviewed by *Ladies Home Journal,* a magazine read by millions of American women, and in the course of it she says that she heard that Princess Diana was getting divorced and she really hopes so because she will be so much happier that way.

So there is forgiveness after all, but guess for whom. You couldn't have it more plain than that. I was slightly stunned myself because, although I think there are many fraudulent things about Mother Teresa, I also think there are many authentic things about her. Anyway, she was forced to issue a statement saying that marriage is God's work and can't be undone and all the usual tripe. But when she was speaking from the heart, she was more forgiving of divorce.

FI: A footnote in your book criticizes Mother Teresa for forgiving *you* for your film about her.

HITCHENS: I said that I didn't ask for forgiveness and I wasn't aware that she could bestow it in any case. Of all the things in the book, that is the one that has attracted most hostile comment—even from friends and people who agree with me. They ask why I object to that, what's wrong with forgiveness? My explanation is that it would be O.K. if she was going to forgive everyone. When she went to Bhopal after the Union Carbide industrial accident killed thousands, she kept saying "Forgive, forgive, forgive." It's O.K. to forgive Union Carbide for its negligence, but for a woman married to an alcoholic child abuser in Ireland who has ten children and no one to look after her, there is *no* forgiveness in this life or the next one. But there is forgiveness for Princess Diana.

FI: There is a Roman Catholic doctrine about the redemption of the soul through suffering. This can be seen in Mother Teresa's work: she thinks suffering is good, and she doesn't use pain relievers in her clinics and so forth. Does she take the same attitude towards her own health? Does she live in accordance with what she preaches?

HITCHENS: I hesitated to cover this in my book, but I decided I had to publish that she has said that the suffering of the poor is something very beautiful and the world is being very much helped by the nobility of this example of misery and suffering.

FI: A horrible thing to say.

HITCHENS: Yes, evil in fact. To say it was unChristian unfortunately would not be true, although many people don't realize that is what Christians believe. It is a positively immoral remark in my opinion, and it should be more widely known than it is.

She is old, she has had various episodes with her own health, and she checks into some of the costliest and finest clinics in the West herself. I hesitated to put that in the book because it seemed as though it would be *ad hominem* (or *ad feminam*) and I try never to do that. I think that the doctrine of hating the sin and loving the sinner is obviously a stupid one, because it's a false antithesis, but a version of it is morally defensible. Certainly in arguments one is only supposed to attack the arguments and not the person presenting them. But the contrast seemed so huge in this case.

It wasn't so much that it showed that her facilities weren't any good, but it showed that they weren't medical facilities at all. There wasn't any place she runs that she could go; as far as I know, their point isn't treatment. And in fairness to her, she has never really claimed that treatment is the point. Although she does accept donations from people who have fooled themselves into thinking so, I haven't found any occasion where she has given a false impression of her work. The only way she could be said to be responsible for spreading it is that she knowingly accepts what comes due to that false impression.

FI: But if people go to her clinics for the dying and they need medical care, does she send them on to the proper places?

HITCHENS: Not according to the testimony of a number of witnesses. I printed the accounts of several witnesses whose testimony I could verify and I've had many other communications from former volunteers in Calcutta and in other missions. All of them were very shocked to find when they got there that they had missed some very crucial point and that very often people who come under the false impression that they would receive medical care are either neglected or given no advice. In other words, anyone going in the hope of alleviation of a serious medical condition has made a huge mistake.

I've got so much testimony from former workers who contacted me after I wrote the book, that I almost have enough material to do a sequel.

11

FI Interview
THE FIRST NEUROPHILOSOPHER: AN INTERVIEW WITH PATRICIA SMITH CHURCHLAND

Pat Churchland is professor of philosophy at the University of California, San Diego, and a humanist laureate of the Academy of Humanism. She is the author of numerous works on philosophy and neuroscience, including Neurophilosophy *(1986, MIT Press) and The* Computational Brain *(1992, MIT Press, with Terrence J. Sejnowski). In this FREE INQUIRY interview, Dr. Churchland discusses modern notions of consciousness, neuroscience, and ethics. It was conducted by David Noelle, president of the San Diego Association of Secular Humanists.—EDS.*

FREE INQUIRY: Pondering the nature of the mind has been a primary occupation of philosophers since the inception of their field. But your approach to the study of thought seems to take you far from the armchair introspections and coffeehouse discussions stereotypically associated with philosophy. In addition to your professorship in the Department of Philosophy, you are a faculty member of the Institute for Neural Computation, you participate in the Cognitive Science Interdisciplinary Program, and you spend much of your time with neuroscientists at the Salk Institute. What has led a philosopher into the laboratory?

PATRICIA CHURCHLAND: The questions that philosophers have been interested in for a long time are the questions that also interest me. I, too, want to understand the nature of consciousness, how it is we perceive, the role of learning and memory, the degree to which emotions play a role in rational decision-making, and so forth. What is new about our time in history is that data from neuroscience and experimental psychology are putting powerful new constraints on our hypotheses. In other words, we now have data that are relevant. My position is really very straightforward. If the data are relevant, then let's take them into account and learn what we can.

Assuming the Greeks to be the fountainhead of modern science and modern philosophy, we see that they were interested in a whole range of questions. They wanted to know the nature of light, what the moon is, what the sun is, why objects in space move, what humans are, and what consciousness is. These were all part of natural philosophy. Many of the questions—the sun, the moon, and what we now call chemical change—have become part of the natural sciences. Only really within this century has it been possible for questions about the nature of humans to become part of a specialized science, namely the science of the mind/brain. Just as earlier questions about astronomy or physics ceased to be "armchair questions," so we are in a transition period where questions about the mind are ceasing to be such.

FI: Do you see yourself as asking the same questions as other philosophers of mind or philosophers of science? Has your interaction with practicing neuroscientists changed the philosophical questions that interest you?

CHURCHLAND: Like Hume or Kant I would very much like to understand the physical basis of consciousness—that is, how it is that out of three pounds of neural tissue there manages to be experiences of pain and colors and so forth. Because psychology and neuroscience have advanced, I have the luxury of considering other specific questions that bear upon the larger problem. For example, it is likely that the intralaminar nucleus of the thalamus plays a special role in consciousness. What really does it project to? Why is it that when it's lesioned, the subject becomes unconscious? What is its special role in coordinating activity in the brain?

FI: When I think of consciousness, it's hard for me to escape the notion of the homunculus—the "inner self" that receives my perceptions and directs my actions. How are modern notions of consciousness different from this naïve view?

CHURCHLAND: First of all, we evidently do have a representation of ourselves as a kind of inner being. That's a representation that brains make, and it probably serves an important role in our cognitive economy. Therefore, it's no surprise that it's hard to get around the feeling that there must be an anatomical correlate of the self. It does look like the activity subserving the representation of self is distributed over a variety of regions. Probably thalamic structures are critical, and probably some cortical structures are critical. Redolfo Llinas and Joe Bogen have the hypothesis that the intralaminar nucleus of the thalamus plays a sort of coordinating role. That's a very plausible hypothesis, and we'll have to see where it goes in the next ten or fifteen years. If they are correct there is a kind of representational structure built up

96

of neuronal activity that is not like a central homunculus and it's not like the pineal gland, but which does seem to play a critical role in awareness.

FI: How does this relate to other findings of localization in the brain? There are known brain centers associated with types of visual processing, with motor responses, and with aspects of language use, to name a few. Do you see this as a kind of localized "seat of consciousness"?

CHURCHLAND: No, not at all. None of those functions that you mentioned are localized in centers as traditionally conceived. Localization implies a task-dedicated, processing-insulated module whose operations are necessary and sufficient for getting a specific job done. It has become very clear in the last decade that that's not the right way to think about brain organization. It does look like there are regions of specialization. We don't know exactly how it is that specialization emerges, on what it depends, and what the limits of plasticity are. In any case, it's pretty clearly not the case that there are regions of localization—that there are modules in that sort of old-fashioned sense.

Redolfo Llinas has suggested that the intralaminar activity provides a context or framework and that the specific sensory thalomo-cortical activity, from vision or from the somatosensory system for example, provides the content. This implies that you need a kind of dialogue between thalamic structures and other structures in order to have awareness. Conscious experience is pretty clearly a phenomenon that involves spatially distributed structures, some of which are especially critical.

FI: Consciousness somehow arises in the interaction of these processes?

CHURCHLAND: Probably. You need visual areas in order to have visual awareness, and you need auditory brain areas intact in order to have auditory awareness, and so on. For sensory perception the corresponding sensory cortices are extremely important. However, there is a kind of misplaced infatuation with cortex as the seat of the soul. Here is a reason for doubting that idea. You can lose huge chunks of cortical structure and have remaining kinds of awareness—somatosensory awareness or awareness of your thoughts. On the other hand, even tiny lesions to the intralaminar nucleus of the thalamus result in a vegetative state.

FI: What role do you think language plays in consciousness? Can one be conscious without language?

CHURCHLAND: Here's where Dan Dennett and I part company. Can you be aware of colors and shapes and sounds and pains and feelings in the absence of language? I can't see why not. We know that aphasic patients who have lost language capacity have sensory experiences as well as thoughts and reflections. We think that preverbal children do, as well. I very much doubt that, with the acquisition of language, sensory data suddenly become conscious. Also, by virtue of similarity in anatomical structure, lots of mammals have largely comparable sensory awareness. They're aware of smells, colors, shapes, pains, and tastes, and so on.

Some studies on humans show that through education and experience you can become aware of things that you weren't aware of before. This is really a matter of extending pattern recognition skills through language-mediated training. You, as a student of neuroscience, will look through a microscope at, say, a cell body of neurons, and you will see mitochondria. You will just look and see them. You won't have to say, "There is this blob of such and such a shape, so that must be mitochrondria." You see the smudge as mitochondria. And, similarly, you hear certain things as bits of language. It's almost unavoidable. So, having experience and culture and having language means that you, of course, do pattern recognition of a very complicated kind.

Perhaps when Dan Dennett says you need language for consciousness, all he means is that you need language to do certain kinds of complex pattern recognition. I doubt even this version. Animals in the wild, who, after all, can have a very tough life and have to be very smart to get around, perform kinds of complex pattern recognition that do not require language. So, my own feeling is that language is very important for lots that humans do, but I don't for a moment think, like Dan Dennett does, that consciousness comes into existence as a virtual machine as you acquire language. I see no evidence. I agree, of course, that there is no homunculus and there is no Cartesian theatre, but Hume taught us that in the eighteenth century.

FI: Has neuroscience taught us anything about our consciousness of our own thoughts and of ourselves?

CHURCHLAND: One of the virtues of Francis Crick's approach is the simple point that you want to start where you can make the most progress. That implies working on sensory awareness before working on abstract thought. The more difficult phenomena will just have to wait until we've uncovered the cards in these basic areas.

Having said that, though, it's certainly very interesting that there are patients like Boswell, who has no hippocampus or autobiographical memory. He doesn't have a sense of himself as a person continuing through time. He has a forty-second time window that he lives in and moves in. Nevertheless, when you meet him, he's personable, charming, and attentive. He uses language, and he interacts well. He makes you feel comfortable. There's no doubt that Boswell has awareness. It shocks the pants off people who think autobiographical memory is necessary for awareness. It's also significant to consider patients who have lost much of their frontal structures. They will show inappropriate emotional inhibition and are unable to plan for the future appropriately. They are unable to delay gratification. But are they conscious? Yes. Not conscious of the importance of making a plan for the future, but certainly conscious of pains, itches, tickles, touches and smells. One point that Antonio Damasio has emphasized, which I think is correct, is that there are probably many aspects to consciousness. Losing some structure, like frontal structure, means that you lose certain consciousness capacities, such as being aware of the importance of the future, but you don't lose awareness of colors. In losing visual cortex you lose the capacity to be aware of colors.

I don't actually know of any lesion where people entirely lose the sense that they are themselves but are otherwise aware. There are lesions in which people are convinced that they're dead, but they still think "I am me." There is also a not uncommon phenomenon in patients with temporal lobe epilepsy, resulting from a car accident, for example, where they display an interesting confluence of traits that weren't seen before. They suddenly become hyper-religious and hyper-graphic. They're constantly writing poems, stories, and letters. They may also become hyper-sexual. Those three features have a tendency to go together. That doesn't mean that there's a physical center for those things, but it is rather remarkable that character traits can be altered in this fashion. Other lesion studies important for the self and self-representation are right parietal lesions, where people tend to neglect, say, the left hemispace and everything in it. I suspect that the representation that the brain builds of the idea that there is "me" is quite deep. Antonio Damasio thinks that self-representation depends on a more basic body representation. We're able to think of ourselves as a "me" because of the way that body representations come into the brain and are integrated. That's quite plausible, actually.

FI: Many people seem to feel threatened by this sort of scientific investigation of consciousness. Some seem to think that such knowledge belittles their self-value. Others see science as threatening their cherished beliefs in substance dualism—in a non-material, and perhaps immortal soul. How have you dealt with such opposition?

CHURCHLAND: Indeed, it's not silly to worry about others controlling our brains. A genuine worry that people have is that, if the workings of the brain are understood in great detail, then others will have access to their private thoughts and may be able to control them. It's extremely unlikely that that could ever happen, given the complexity of the brain, but people need to be reassured that it is unlikely. Given that complexity, the most we can realistically aim for is a grasp of the general principles of brain function—not to be able to predict, moment by moment, what somebody else will do.

The further issue has to do with what all this implies for a non-physical soul. I'm inclined to say that it certainly seems to me improbable. This view raises some very deep questions about how to live a life. Probably, as it is suggested in Ecclesiastes, for example, we need to make the very best of life, here. Many people do feel we should have something beyond us that is greater than us. Of course, there is something beyond us and that is greater than us and, in a way, that's the planet, or, if you like, the universe as a whole, toward which, I think, it's possible to have very rich feelings of belonging and care. Feelings that often get funneled into very specific metaphysical ideas can actually be funneled as easily into care for others in the human community, the biotic community, or for the planet itself. Rather than expecting that the wrongs will be made right in the hereafter, we need to care very much about we do right here.

That's usually my response to worries about the mind as brain-dependent. It's useful to remind people, too, that even something like the Bible is not univocal on the issue of an afterlife. Ecclesiastes is one example of a book where the message is much more like the message of secular humanism: do good works, make a decent life for yourself, think about what you're doing, and try to behave wisely.

This humanizing side of science needs emphasis. One only needs to think about, say, the example of anaesthesia. When anaesthetics were first discovered, many people, and the Catholic church in particular, were deeply opposed to their use on the grounds that they were unnatural. These were tools of the devil! Pain was what God intended. Pain was part of life and had to be suffered. Now, we look back on that position with utter disbelief. How could having a leg amputated without anaesthetic be good for one's character? I think that similar humanizing results will emerge with greater understanding of what makes us what we are. But, as with any science, one also has to bear in mind that there can be misuses. As a rational caring community, we have to see to it that rules are in place, that decency and civility are honored, and that science is not turned to evil uses.

FI: Has neuroscientific research contributed to our understanding of ethics and ethical reasoning?

CHURCHLAND: One of the very important developments that has emerged from the Damasios's work in Iowa City does bear upon ethics and decision-making. In particular, lesion data strongly suggest that emotion and feelings are essential components of rational decision-making. Consequently, early education to engender the appropriate socialized feelings is extremely important. When the circuitry is gummed up or is absent due to some sort of fetal abnormality or through an accident, then the ability to feel remorse is lost. We have to take very good care that those people don't run amok. The capacity to learn civility seems to be innate, and the relevant circuitry can be destroyed.

The other point is something that I owe to Paul Churchland. We teach complex pattern recognition to children as they grow up. We teach them to recognize certain paradigm situations as "unfair" and then they extrapolate from that. An important part of teaching pattern recognition is not just the purely cognitive aspects, but that the right emotions are felt.

Aristotle isn't sexy and glamorous. He doesn't have an outlandish theory of knowledge politics that Plato does. As a freshman one reads Plato and says, "Wow! This is so cool! This is really wild! I never thought about this before!" Then one reads Aristotle and thinks, "This guy sounds like my Dad. That can't be very interesting." But over the long haul you realize that the much deeper, much more insightful, much more sensible position is Aristotle's.

I think we need a rethinking—a sort of bringing up to date—of Aristotelian ideas about socialization, politics, ethics, and so forth. It's not glamorous, it's just very sensible. If you think of the neo-Nazis on one side and the "woo-woo" postmodernists on the other, it's very possible to see Aristotle as giving you a very sensible alternative. You can be a realist about some things and a relativist about others. You can be sensible about ethics without being doctrinaire. You can see the importance of knowledge in making ethical decisions and in development of ethical wisdom and ethical understanding, but without being an absolutist or Gospel-truther. There is a really interesting confluence between Aristotle and our modern understanding, from within psychology and neuroscience, of the way the brain actually works.

FI: At least part of the story of the Damasios's studies seems to be that ethical decision-making involves more than cold, unfeeling rational thought.

CHURCHLAND: Absolutely! One of the interesting results, actually, of modern neuroscience is that we can see that Kant was wrong when he claimed that the most moral character is the one who strips away all emotion, all feeling, and is purely rational. Those are the people who *can't* make good ethical decisions. Of course, it drives the philosophers up the wall when I say, "We now think that there is empirical reason to show that Kant was just flatly wrong. Hume was right, and Kant was wrong. There's a result." But I think it's true. There's much more to say about that story, and about how cognition and emotion need to interact, the role of early education, what this biasing really comes to in neurobiological terms, the role of logic and mathematics, and so on. But, pure reason unfettered by emotion? No.

FI: This naturalistic view of ethical reasoning seems to run counter to the popular religious views in which proper behavior is legislated by a divine authority.

CHURCHLAND: How lovely it would be if life were simple enough such that a set of rules could suffice as a moral-behavior algorithm. Alas, as Socrates made painfully clear, one of life's tough realities is that, however morality is based, it is not on any set of rules that can be reliably followed to always guarantee the correct choice. The Ten Commandments can give us a rough guide. The Koran or the ideas of Chief Seattle or Confucius all can give us rough guides. Problems inevitably arise, however, because there is no rule for telling us when morality requires a departure from an edict, such as "Tell the truth" or "Thou shalt not kill," or what to do when edicts conflict. As with the development of any kind of understanding about the world, common sense seems fundamentally important in developing moral understanding. In the moral domain, common sense seems to be a blend of instinctual sympathy (Hume's moral sentiment) and experience-dependent understanding (Aristotle's practical wisdom). Our feelings are some guide, but they can lead us astray. Our reason is some guide, but it needs the balance of feeling and the breadth of experience. As we understand more about how brains work, we shall likely achieve new insights about human needs, choices, and springs of action. Such knowledge will not by itself solve ethical problems, but it may help as we struggle to develop a more adequate moral understanding.

We invite you to become an Associate Member of the

As an Associate Member you will receive four issues a year of the new *Secular Humanist Bulletin*. The *Bulletin* keeps you up-to-date on humanist news, issues and activities, and provides a forum for members to share ideas and plans.

Other benefits you will receive as an Associate Member include:
- **10% discount on registration fees for conferences and seminars**
- **10% discount on audiotapes and videotapes**
- **10% discount on a select range of humanist and freethought books**
- **10% discount on secular humanist T-shirts and other merchandise**
- ***Family Matters* four times a year**
- **Your personalized membership card**

☐YES, I wish to support the work of the Council for Secular Humanism by becoming an Associate Member

Enclosed are my dues for:

☐Annual Individual Membership $20   ☐Annual Family Membership $34
☐Two-year Individual Membership $36   ☐Two-year Family Membership $54
☐Three-year Individual Membership $49   ☐Three-year Family Membership $78
☐Lifetime Associate Membership $1,000 (Life members also receive FREE INQUIRY for life.)

☐Check or money order enclosed

Charge my ☐VISA☐MasterCard #_____ Exp._____

Signature _____

Name _____ Daytime Phone # _____

Address _____

City _____ State _____ Zip_____

Return to: Council Memberships, Box 664, Amherst, NY 14226-0664
Or call toll-free 800-458-1366. Fax charges to: 716-636-1733.